ABOUT THE AUTHOR

C000116578

Anne Dickson is a freelanc[e]
trainer. She is recognised as a leading authority on women's
development, assertiveness training and interactive
communication. Her bestselling, widely translated *A Woman
In Your Own Right* (Quartet, 1982) has become the core
textbook for assertiveness trainers throughout the world.
Together with *Assert Yourself*, a television series based on her
book, it has helped to make the skills available to a wide
number of people.

Her second book, *The Mirror Within* (Quartet, 1984), arose
from her work as a psychosexual counsellor, working within
group and individual contexts, over the past twenty-two
years.

Both aspects of her work as an educator have contained
an emotional component because she has always been
committed to the management of emotion in an everyday
rather than clinical environment.

TRUSTING THE TIDES

Self-Empowerment through our Emotions

Anne Dickson

RIDER
LONDON · SYDNEY · AUCKLAND · JOHANNESBURG

This book is dedicated, with love,
to those who have the courage to live a heartful life.

1 3 5 7 9 10 8 6 4 2

Copyright © Anne Dickson 2000

Anne Dickson has asserted her right to be identified as the Author of this work in accordance with the Copyright, Designs and Patents Act, 1988.

First published in 2000 by Rider,
an imprint of Ebury Press, Random House,
20 Vauxhall Bridge Road, London SW1V 2SA
www.randomhouse.co.uk

Random House Australia (Pty) Limited
20 Alfred Street, Milsons Point, Sydney,
New South Wales 2061, Australia

Random House New Zealand Limited
18 Poland Road, Glenfield,
Auckland 10, New Zealand

Random House South Africa (Pty) Limited
Endulini, 5A Jubilee Road,
Parktown 2193, South Africa

The Random House Group Limited Reg. No. 954009

Papers used by Rider are natural, recyclable products made from wood grown in sustainable forests.

Printed and bound by Mackays of Chatham plc, Kent

A CIP catalogue record for this book
is available from the British Library

ISBN 0-7126-0547-9

Contents

List of figures   vi
Acknowledgements   vii
Introduction   ix

Part One
Shaping the Emotional Landscape

1   Cultural legacy: myths and assumptions about
    emotions   3
2   Bearings – the emotional compass   10
3   Heartscape   26
4   Processing emotion in our early years   43
5   Sequence: emergence and arousal   51
6   Sequence: release and resolution   58
7   Inhibition and obstruction   63
8   Restimulation   72
9   Formation of survival patterns   83

Part Two
A New Approach: DANCE

Introduction   105
10 Distress v. Denial   109
11 Acknowledgement v. Rationalisation   111
12 Naming v. Evasion   122
13 Catharsis v. Accumulation   129
14 Evaluation v. Distortion   136

Part Three
The Mind–Body Link in Everyday Life

Introduction   145
15 How emotions affect the mind   149
16 How emotions affect the body   154
17 Living the mind–body link   166
18 Momentum: the impulse of emotion   185

Appendix   190
Index   194

List of figures

1   The ocean floor: three fundamental needs
2   The ocean: emotional currents between the three polarities
3   The three polarities
4   A child's experience of the three polarities
5   Emotional arousal
6   Emotional release
7   Blocked emotional arousal
8   Emotion blocked in the body
9   Emotion as medium
10   The wheel
11   The wheel with grief at the hub
12   The wheel with anger at the hub
13   The wheel with fear at the hub
14   The wheel: interweaving patterns
15   Kites

Acknowledgements

For me, one of the best things about writing a book is that I have the opportunity to thank publicly some of the people I most love and care for.

The ten years it has taken me to complete this book have seen much change and loss in my personal life: one person who has been significant throughout that time is Liz Clasen who, apart from being my dear and most enduring friend, has helped and sustained me in her professional capacity as ongoing editor. Halfway through this period, I met Carol Davis. She has been a source of support and comfort during some very dark times and her own insights and wisdom have found their way onto these pages. Barbara Elliott, a rare friend who truly sees me, has also contributed her invaluable professional and personal perceptions of the content of the book.

Loneliness is integral to the writing process but at times, when it became acute enough to render me unproductive, I had to find a temporary refuge that could provide me with the company and congeniality for me to continue. I would like to thank those who cared for me in their homes for a while so that I could work: Stanley Jepson and Liz Clasen; David and Barbara Elliott; Kirsten Rudbeck; my brother Graeme, his wife Alison and their family.

Nikki Henriques has helped me from afar with homoeopathy and steady care; Paola Russell sustained me, at a crucial time, with massage and thought-provoking conversation about various chapters.

Research into other fields leaves me indebted to Terry Looker of Manchester Metropolitan University who generously shared his expertise; Thomas Nielson of the University of Arhus whose paper I found extremely helpful; and Frances Norton of St James Library at the University of Leeds who took a lot of time to help me research into the literature on psychosomatic illness.

Computer literacy still evades me but for help in the early days I would like to thank Peter Coulson for responding with patient assistance to my alarm calls; also John Elkins who helped me with similar problems and took the time to read and comment on a section of the manuscript.

Once again, Stella Salem helped with typing early drafts; so did Karen Wood and Pat Hicks. To these three, my sincere thanks.

I'd like to thank Clare Manifold for her comments in the earliest stages, Kay Barwick and Breda Hill for their support and Caroline Raymond of Stress in Perspective for her help. Also Judy Moore, whose encouragement and suggestions came as a breath of fresh air last year, inspiring me to reorder the final structure of the book.

Jenny Russell contributed her unique blend of challenge, inquiry and commitment to detail during the perilous final stages; her companionship over this period was generously offered and much appreciated.

Finally I want to thank those who have helped less directly but have been an essential part of this project. John Heron taught me co-counselling twenty-two years ago; he later became a friend and colleague and I have always remained grateful for being able to learn those skills from such an excellent teacher and guide. More recently, David Elliott has given generously of his knowledge, experience and innate shrewdness about the publishing world.

Participants in my classes and courses over the years have been a constant source of inspiration. Together with friends and colleagues, they have often urged me to keep going – I would like to thank them all for their written and spoken words of support, their beams and their prayers.

Introduction

THE roots of this book lie in my personal experience. I am an ordinary human being, born into an ordinary family, in what were, halfway through the century, ordinary circumstances. My own recollection of family life is of little closeness; although we shared occasions of pleasure and celebration, frustration and sadness, there was little real openness.

Feelings were not talked about. Childhood expressions of tears and rage were strongly discouraged and, in adulthood, any emotional expression was suitably muted. Occasional outbursts were treated as temporary lapses of control and explained away as the consequences of too much to drink or pressure of work or mysterious problems that couldn't be discussed.

Like many other children, I could detect a lot of emotion between my parents, and between us, their four children, which was all the more powerful for the lack of open discussion. I had no name for these undercurrents; I simply sensed them. This lack of acknowledgement of feelings contrasted strongly with the intensity evident in voices and eyes, and left me bewildered and disturbed.

We experienced life's usual ups and downs; between us, we also encountered problems of alcoholism, redundancy, teenage pregnancy and abortion, depression and anorexia, and still nobody referred to feelings. Even when hospital treatment was sought for help, emotional concerns were entirely absent from the professional medical agenda, so we handled these phenomena in our familiar muted fashion.

In early adulthood, I emerged as a hard-working and committed teacher, but I was unprepared for emotional intimacy. I regularly used alcohol to anaesthetise my anxieties, to gag the voices of self-criticism and, occasionally, to fuel aggressive outbursts and release of tension.

A turning point occurred around my twenty-ninth birthday when I was introduced to a set of skills that proved vital for me and certainly life-changing. For the first time in my adult life, I was presented with the opportunity to explore, express and learn to release my feelings in a safe and structured context.

Slowly and with regular and committed practice, I learned to trust my body's responses. Emotional release became and remains an inevitable and natural function in my life. Without this facility, I am certain I would have had to resort to medication to get through periods of depression in the past fifteen years and, like many other people, would be unable to function without it.

This learning has consistently underpinned all my teaching, training and counselling work of the past twenty-three years. Whether working in the context of assertiveness training or psychosexual counselling, the programmes I have evolved have always had an integral emotional component. This is because feelings, expressed or unexpressed, conscious or unconscious, lie at the heart of nearly every difficulty – whether it is a problem in communicating assertively or an apparent sexual difficulty. What has fascinated me time after time is that participants in my programmes have always been extremely interested in finding out the why, the where, the what, and the how of emotions – but have not known where to look for this information.

Few adults with whom I have met and worked, whatever their personal qualities or professional experience, have any real idea about how emotions function. We remain, so to speak, emotionally illiterate. It is hard to find the words to describe our feelings: we find it difficult to distinguish between sentimental tears, manipulative tears and the real thing; we confuse anger with aggression, grief with depression. We suffer from all sorts of bodily ailments that we *know* deep down are connected with feelings, but cannot understand what is happening. We know that tears are natural but feel desperately embarrassed when we cry. Without information, we remain fearful. Our feelings become trapped in the realm of the unknown and the mysterious. And yet I believe that many people want to understand their emotions better.

Talking and writing about emotion clinically is like describing the chemical composition of seawater or analysing the depth of ocean currents. Neither description, although accurate, conveys the subjective experience of the taste or feel or sensation of being immersed in the water. On the other hand, talking and writing about emotion *emotionally*, in a way truer to the subject matter, risks presenting the reader with a sentimental and confusing mess.

This book is a guide to our feelings, charting the currents and movements of the heart. It answers the why, the where, the what, of emotions and explains how we can manage our feelings more effectively. Above all, it makes clear that emotion is part of everyday life and need not be seen as a problem.

It is our insistence on emotions as problematic that accounts for our growing dependence on ranks of professionals – psychologists, psychiatrists, therapists and counsellors – whose expertise is relied upon to diagnose the 'fault' and correct it. Sometimes the experience of counselling and therapy will teach us about our emotions, but not necessarily.

Experience has convinced me that understanding how our emotions affect us is as important as understanding how our digestion and respiration function. There is no need to be an expert any more than we need to be a dietician or lung specialist in order to exercise some choice about what we eat or how we breathe.

What follows is based on fifty years' personal experience, modified, clarified and enhanced by twenty years' professional experience of working directly and indirectly with other people and their emotions.

There should perhaps be a warning here: some of the content of this book is emotionally explicit! Exploration of emotion is not possible without occasionally touching on aspects of personal experience – realisations, memories, associations – that may be uncomfortable, even painful for the reader. Eventually, though, with information and recognition come an acceptance and increased trust of the process of our emotions.

Trusting the Tides is intended as both a theoretical and a practical guide to our emotions. The first part offers a theory of emotion and explains how our experience of and learning about emotion as children establishes the patterns of our adult behaviour and relationships. It explains the emergence, arousal and release of emotion as a natural process and shows how our beliefs and fears obstruct this process so that unexpressed emotion often disrupts our lives in various ways. Part Two explores the potential for practical change: how to remedy and improve emotional education; how to establish emotional literacy, how to express feelings more clearly and also the possibility of more radically healing some of the effects of past emotional obstruction. The third part shows how we can live with the mind–body link at a practical level, and the relevance of emotional management in everyday life.

Remember, the medium of emotion is not entirely new to us. This basic guide also serves as a reminder – we may no longer be able to speak the language of emotion with fluency and confidence but it is, nevertheless, a language that every one of us once knew by heart.

A practical note

At the end of most chapters is a section containing suggestions and exercises. This enables readers, if they are interested, to take the information in the previous chapter a stage further, and to use this book not only for reflection and reference but as a workbook for individual and personal exploration.

The suggestions can be followed on your own but I would strongly recommend sharing the exercises with a trusted other person. This is the context for which they have been designed. Although it is helpful to reflect privately, the prevailing invisibility of emotion, and the anticipation of aloneness and anxiety when we explore this dimension of our lives, make it especially valuable to communicate and share our findings with somebody else. In this way, too, it can be a lot more fun.

If you decide to do this, you may find it useful to read *Setting the Scene* in the Appendix beforehand.

Part One

SHAPING THE EMOTIONAL LANDSCAPE

1 | Cultural legacy: myths and assumptions about emotions

THE various words we use to describe the life of the heart each convey a slightly different meaning. **Emotion** contains a sense of motion: being moved by a gesture, an image, a sound, a realisation, so that our relation to our world is somehow changed. There is a kaleidoscopic shift. If the emotion is experienced as pleasurable we move towards the source; if the experience is hurtful or threatening, we move away from it.

The word **feeling** conveys the dimension of sensation, literally keeping us in touch with our world. Just as, with our eyes closed, our fingers can differentiate between the texture, shape and temperature of different objects, so our feelings give us immediate information about our environment. This medium of experience is as vital for survival and growth as our capacity for intellectual discrimination.

A less used word is **affect.** Affect describes the way in which we are ourselves changed by or change others through emotional experience. The word **mood** and the more old-fashioned word **humour** also belong here: these words describe a temporary or permanent emotional 'climate' which we sense around ourselves or others.

Passion is a word that encompasses both power and suffering. Emotions are powerful forces capable of urging us beyond rational endeavour. The arousal of passion, for example, in response to unrequited or lost love, is also associated with great pain.

Last, a word that is often misunderstood is **sentiment**. Sentiment is one step removed from direct emotional experience – it literally means bringing the feeling to mind. A grandmother's ring has sentimental value because it reminds us of the emotions we felt towards her and of what she represented. A sentimental journey brings to mind feelings connected to past experiences. Greetings cards depicting small furry animals or rose-covered cottages are designed specifically to induce sentiment – to bring to mind emotions associated with those particular images. Sentiment is to real emotion as a TV soap is to actual experience – it is a way of feeling by proxy, a method of stirring feelings. It should not be confused with the real thing.

We inherit from the culture into which we are born a particular way of seeing the world around us. What concerns us here is the way we have been conditioned to look at things as being split into either/or, good/bad, black/white, because the way we look at emotion is no exception.

Emotional segregation

We have learned to look at emotion as either positive or negative. This is so automatic, that if asked to make an instant list of positive and negative feelings we would probably end up with words such as love, joy, happiness, confidence, contentment on the positive side, and sadness, frustration, anger, anxiety, on the negative side. If challenged about this division we might well insist that this demarcation is obvious, that happiness feels better than loneliness, that grief never feels enjoyable, and who on earth has ever looked forward to feeling anxiety?

It is extremely difficult to believe, but although this is certainly our experience, it need not be so. In fact, the positive/negative categorisation is an imposition deeply embedded in our culture over thousands of years and its influence is therefore impossible to avoid. Nevertheless, it remains a way of seeing which has been imposed from outside. Part of the reason why anxiety feels unpleasant, is because we expect it to feel unpleasant; because we associate certain feelings with negativity, they become known as negative feelings.

It is impossible to overestimate the impact of growing up in an environment that taught us feelings were either good or bad. The first major consequence is that good feelings have become desirable and bad feelings have become undesirable, according to a code of moral and medical correctness. A good feeling such as love is desirable because it has a good effect on others, shows us in a socially acceptable light, and is good for us physically. Anger, on the other hand, has a detrimental effect on others, shows us in an unpleasant light socially, and is bad for our health.

One consequence of this division is that the value of anger as an emotion has disappeared, while the pursuit of happiness and love has become paramount. We suffer agonies of self-repression in order to deny feelings of anger because they suggest a moral failing, whereas the achievement of happiness is an extraordinarily seductive goal implying the proper state to which we are entitled. Feelings of frustration, uncertainty or grief are assumed to be bad and, we hope, only temporary, because we believe we should be having good, positive, happy feelings instead.

This notion of desirable and undesirable feelings generates a cultural momentum of its own. Enormous amounts of time, energy and money are poured into making people feel happier, whether it be through psychotherapy, money-making schemes, exercise routines to reduce stress, or strong liquor to take the edge off things.

As a result, most of us are unable to recognise and acknowledge feelings precisely because we have learned to censor ourselves. We have learned to ignore or hide or bury certain feelings because we believe them to be negative and therefore undesirable. It has become easier to acknowledge only positive feelings.

A second consequence of this negative/positive division is an imposed belief that emotions operate in mutually exclusive units. We believe that the feeling of anger is contradictory to the feeling of love – we believe that anxiety and confidence are at opposite ends of the spectrum. This either/or division does not stand up in reality because we know from experience that emotions co-exist. It is certainly possible to feeling anger and love towards someone at the same moment. It is possible to feel angry and loving towards a close friend; to feel simultaneous grief and relief, for example, after the death of someone whom you loved dearly but who was in a lot of pain or whose death also signified the end of a huge burden of responsibility.

Addressing a large audience, anticipating a birth or abseiling for the first time might elicit parallel feelings of anxiety and excitement. A loving gesture can prompt an immediate feeling of sadness, as well as joy and delight. It is no accident that tears express both happiness and sadness, or that laboratory research indicates that physiological arousal is virtually identical whether the subject is anxious or angry. This either/or distinction is simply imposed from the outside in an attempt to order the apparent chaos of emotional reality, but it only confuses us more.

A third consequence of categorising one large area of emotion as undesirable is the belief that a bad emotion acts like a virus. Fear of contamination in western culture at large has led to the isolation and 'quarantine' of those labelled mentally ill or psychiatrically disturbed. Although there are valid reasons why some people would be better restrained 'for their own good', this fear of rampant disease is never far away.

Individuals describe their hurt and surprise when friends, neighbours, even relatives, avoid contact with them after they have experienced a death, divorce, redundancy or some such personal trauma. Helplessness and fear of being drawn in and caught up in others' 'undesirable' feelings prompt us to shield ourselves, so we avoid others or withdraw from them. At the very time that people are most in need of a little care and space in which to talk, when they need their loss or anger acknowledged in order to come to terms with a new reality, social constraints encourage them to hide their feelings as an unsightly affliction or disguise them with a superficial and acceptable veneer.

Even without external disapproval we can find it difficult to admit that we experience unacceptable feelings, however sympathetic the listener. Anyone who has witnessed the struggle of an individual to acknowledge the so-called 'negative' feelings of envy, hate and despair will recognise the agony involved, and if you have ever tried to do so yourself you will know how hard it is.

The attempt to express and therefore to admit to 'negative' feelings puts us in the front line of the battle between reason and emotion. In the contest between the rational and the emotional it is not hard to identify which has come to be considered as the superior and preferable force. Preference for the rational runs along familiar lines:

'I'm talking about *facts* here, I'm not interested in your feelings.'
'Can't we just discuss this rationally?'
'Now do *try* to be reasonable!'

Yet the power of emotion is considerable and not easily subdued. Since we seem unable to make emotion go away, we try to make sense of it in the hope that analysis will lead to comprehension; that comprehension will lead to control; that control will reduce the threat of potential chaos. We insist on contemplating and assessing emotion through rational eyes:

'There is no reason at all to behave like that!'

'I can't understand what she's got to be depressed about – she's got a good husband, lovely children, nice house . . .'

'Who'd have thought he'd do something like that – always seemed such a reasonable fellow!'

Another way we rationalise emotion is by following unwritten rules for expression. There are clear demarcation lines: which emotion is permissible, when, where, by whom, and in what manner. A woman attending her husband's funeral may be allowed to express grief, which would be seemly, with a few tears, but no loud sobbing, hysteria or excessive expression, which would be *un*seemly. On the occasion of his father's death, a man would also be allowed tears but would have no permission for rage at his dead father, who may have abused him terribly. First of all, rage would be out of place. Secondly, it would be considered more properly confined to the privacy of our own home, or preferably to the consulting room of the local psychiatrist. Even the appropriate emotion of grief has a time limit and shouldn't exceed a decent mourning period:

'Isn't it time she got over that by now?'

'You're not still dwelling on it all, are you? Can't you make more of an effort?'

'Why don't you just try for another child/ get another dog?'

One of the aspects of feeling we get misled by is the belief that some nationalities are 'emotional' and others are not. It is true that there are obvious cultural differences: each culture has its own rules of social acceptability. An Irish wake may be known for its latitude of expression and openness to celebration as well as grief. The Americans have a reputation for being more extrovert at public gatherings, the Italians for 'showing their feelings' at the drop of a hat. The sounds of collective mourning at funerals in African or Arabic countries contrast sharply with the more subdued occasions in other cultures.

These are merely differences in cultural tolerance of emotional *display*. There is no deeper implication that the individuals within these cultures are more familiar or more comfortable with the expression or communication of deep emotion than those of us brought up in a more reserved tradition. Alcohol and other drugs are used to deaden and suppress feelings in many countries, regardless of the evident cultural differences.

When I work with individuals, I find that the extremes of this rational/emotional polarity are evident in their imaginations even if they don't put these thoughts into words. Emotion has drawn unto itself messy, childish, primitive, weak, ugly, treacherous and dark associations. Reason, on the other hand, has fastidiously divested itself of these qualities in favour of order, civility, stability, nobility, security and enlightenment.

Even though we know these things intellectually, we do not stop being afraid of the power of emotion. Our reluctance to open the can is evidence of the worms we anticipate within. We numb our fear with all sorts of substances, we push emotion back down our throats with food, we distract ourselves with obsessive activity or we lash out with words or fists, in the hope that transferring the pain will lessen our own.

Counteracting the negativity of emotion from a position of fear involves an exhausting struggle. We listen, observe, advise, interpret, analyse and tie up unwanted feelings in strait-jackets. We render them powerless with strong medication, even surgically remove those parts of the body that appear to cause them. We lock up unwanted feelings, we punish and banish them. Ultimately, we bury them in the cold dead ground of denial.

And yet with information and understanding to stand alongside our fear, it *is* possible to trust and value our emotions and to become as familiar and easy with our emotional behaviour as we are with the rational side of ourselves. But until we can make more sense of emotion, we will continue to be mistrustful. Making sense of emotion is what this book is about.

◆ Make a list of what you would label 'positive' and 'negative' feelings.

◆ In the positive list, are there any feelings that you recognise pretending to feel, or wish you could feel, instead of what you actually feel? Make a note of them.

◆ In the negative list, are there any feelings that induce shame/guilt/ fear/embarrassment? Do you have difficulty acknowledging any feeling on this list, to yourself or to anybody else?

◆ Have you ever found it necessary to numb your feelings in some way? If so, how? You may recognise that some feelings make you compensate by excessive activity, e.g. over-eating, over-drinking, over-working. Or you may find that any emotional arousal makes you take evasive action. What are your personal strategies for dealing with emotion?

2 | Bearings – the emotional compass

FEAR of emotion creates a vicious circle: it prevents us from getting proper information, and lack of information increases our fear. This chapter offers a theoretical chart to help us become acquainted with the currents of the heart so that we can begin to feel more familiar and less uncertain.

Most of us are puzzled about where feelings actually come from. We can be feeling reasonably calm one moment then, suddenly, we feel tearful without any apparent cause. We think we have long recovered from a deep loss when, without warning, it hits us again. Or when someone makes a remark, insignificant in itself, which causes us to react with disproportionate fury, we know we are over-reacting, but can't seem to stop ourselves.

This sense of being ambushed by feelings contributes to our uneasiness about emotions. We often feel at the mercy of our emotions instead of being in control of them. Instead of responding appropriately, we spend a lot of time regretting an excess of expression or wishing instead that we could have been less inhibited with our anger, love or gratitude towards someone. So, feelings appear mysterious, unpredictable and dangerous. Dangerous because once we give way to pressure and vent just a little, before we know where we are, we're disgorging a torrent of abuse or drowning in floods of tears and, for a while, it is impossible to regain equilibrium. It's hard to get on with ordinary life because we feel overwhelmed.

Mysterious, unpredictable, dangerous and uncontrollable – it is hardly surprising that this is an area we are reluctant to explore. As a consequence, our understanding of emotion is fairly crude and simplistic. We associate grief with loss, anger with frustration, and joy with love. Although we are made aware of the more subtle nuances of emotion through the work of artists, there usually remains a gap between the awareness of poetic or literary evocation and its practical relevance to our day-to-day lives. Let's look at a map of the terrain beneath the waters – the ocean floor so to speak.

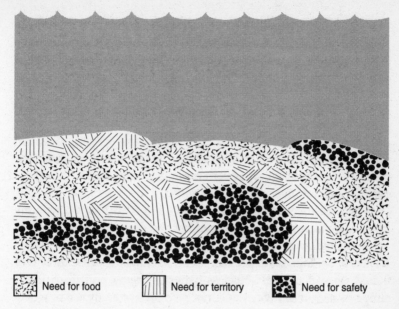

Need for food   Need for territory   Need for safety

Figure 1   *The ocean floor: three fundamental needs*

I find it useful to picture the terrain as formed from three over-lapping yet distinct and differently-coloured strata that represent the three basic areas of emotion. These three areas of colour show a multitude of depths and intensities and differing shades where they meet one another, blending to produce a 'marbled' effect.

This terrain represents what can be called the animal, instinctual, primitive aspects, the deepest part of ourselves which constitutes the bedrock of our emotional being. The determining impulse is to continue life in the threat of death and the strata relate to survival: the need for food, the need to establish territory and the need for safety. Food and shelter are necessary for the maintenance of the organism, the need to establish territory and safety from harm are both vital for continuing survival.

Each basic need promotes the acquisition of appropriate skills. First, animals need to know what to eat and where to find it: they need to keep close to the supply of sustenance and to signal their hunger. Second, they need to learn boundaries – a territorial learning through which a creature acquires the skill of distinguishing self from others. It learns rules of hierarchy within the family group. It learns when to submit or attack and how to respond in a way that will offer the best chance of its own survival. These needs demand skills of communication: recognition and imitation of a range of signals, smells, sounds, movements, gestures – a rudimentary language that helps any creature to recognise its own kind, to distinguish friend from foe, and to learn where it will be safe.

All three needs are interdependent: the more food available, the fitter the animal in defence; the more effectively it can communicate, the greater the likelihood of obtaining food and protecting itself. Left in conditions which are natural for that species, an animal will bond with a parent or others of its own kind and will learn the complex communication system necessary to maintain the whole cycle of generation and regeneration.

When these needs are not met or are impeded in some way, the physiological response of the animal corresponds to a primitive emotion: loss, anger or fear. As a complex and hidebound human, I marvel at an animal's expression of fear or anger because there is of course no gap of consciousness between trigger and response. It simply *is* its fear or rage. It does not restrain it or analyse it or worry about what the neighbours might think.

In infant human behaviour, we find a similar lack of self-con-

Figure 2   *The ocean: emotional currents between the three polarities*

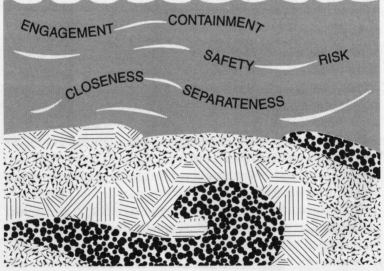

 Need for food   Need for territory   Need for safety

sciousness, as regards instinctual needs for nourishment, territory and safety; psychological development begins very early. Given the long period of dependency of the human infant, the bodily needs of early childhood are synonymous with emotional needs. This means being fed is being loved; being untouched is being unloved. The separation between body and mind comes later.

Our bodily needs remain for the rest of our lives but they become more complex and sophisticated as we develop emotionally and intellectually. The need for food and physical maintenance broadens to include the emotional need for love and closeness; the need to establish physical territory develops into the need to establish psychological boundaries; along with the need for physical safety, develops the emotional need for trust.

Each of these human needs is balanced by an opposing need of equally vital importance, forming three polarities: the need for *closeness* is balanced by the need for *separateness*; the need for *engagement* is balanced by the need for *containment*; the need for *safety* is balanced by the need for *risk*. These opposing yet complementary needs form three polarities which are crucial to understanding the basis of emotion.

Let's look at each in turn.

Closeness ⟵————————⟶ Separateness

The needs for closeness and separateness are equally important. We move between the two depending on our needs at different times of our lives. The infant needs nurture for emotional survival. It also needs to develop a sense of self. The to and fro between the needs is evident throughout childhood and adolescence. The child needs to assert himself as an individual, wanting to manage on his own, going off to explore and then coming back to seek reassurance. The teenager who wants to do her own thing, to make her own mark as far removed from her parents as possible also needs to be sure they are still there when she needs them.

Throughout adulthood we can see the same rhythm. The need for intimacy reflects both the giving and receiving of care and love in all forms. There are times when we want someone to talk to and share a happy or difficult experience. We long to be close, to be held, to make love, to share in the magic dynamics of give and take, of a meeting of minds, touching of hearts, those moments of wordless communion of heart or mind or soul. We want to embrace and lose ourselves in someone else.

Experiences that meet our need for closeness include:

Being listened to and heard
Companionship
A meeting of minds
Sharing food, experiences, sexual pleasure
Receiving and giving praise or sympathy
A small hand slipping into yours
Preparing a loving surprise for someone
Soothing away someone's aches and pains
Sharing a hug
Being a willing audience of one

The emotions associated with this first polarity are based in **love** and **grief**. If our need for closeness is met in any of these or other ways, our response is based in the emotion of love with associated feelings such as joy, tenderness, care, contentment, warmth, happiness.

The need for love is obvious, but the complementary need for separateness may come as more of a surprise. More often than not, we are encouraged and conditioned to regard only the first of these needs as significant. Cultural pressure to be part of a couple and a sense of social failure if we are not in a relationship underpin the flourishing commerce of dating agencies and small ads offering opportunities to find our 'other half'. There is no guidance or encouragement in western culture to develop the facility of being alone and separate. Nevertheless, this impulse remains as vital in the human being as the need for love shared with others. There are times when we long to be alone, to find peace and quiet and to get back to ourselves; to pull up the drawbridge, close the door, find time to clear out the inter-personal clutter, in order to regain our internal integrity and balance.

We will and do find ways of meeting this need, often without being conscious of it.

Experiences that meet our need for separateness include:

Pottering in the garden shed
'Cutting off' from a situation
Taking the dog for a walk

Reading the newspaper
Absorption in a television programme, a book or in music
Going for a bicycle ride
Going for a run
Going to the local
Finding a reason to take to your bed

If the need for separateness is fulfilled, our emotions will be similar to those that arise in response to the fulfilment of the need for closeness: love, joy, satisfaction and contentment. There is a sense of coming home, getting back to 'base', a joyful reunion, a pleasure of settling back into our own skin – one that fits perfectly. There is a feeling of love and compassion towards our own being.

To manage our feelings effectively, it is essential to understand the connection between the need and its associated emotions. Meeting these needs, as in the above examples, will elicit feelings associated with love; blocking the need will elicit its complementary emotion of grief. What happens when our needs for closeness and separateness are not met? How does this happen?

Experiences that block our need for closeness include:

Bereavement
Withdrawal of someone close to us
Separation from loved ones
The end of a relationship
Being unable to confide in someone
Living alone
An important loss
Excessive criticism
Being touched without care
Rejection

When we experience this need being blocked, the spectrum of emotions based in *grief* ranges from sadness and hurt to sorrow and desolation.

Experiences that block our need for separateness include:

Over-interference by a partner or friends
Attention to others' needs taking up every minute of the day

Over-stimulation
Lack of silence
Lack of being because of over-doing
Constantly having to fulfil the demands of different roles
Always having to give an account of ourselves
Unwilling participation in sexual activity
Never being able to enjoy solitude without feeling lonely

When our need for separateness is unmet or denied, we experience a similar sadness and sense of loss. These feelings are less easily described because our focus is usually on what we feel in relation to loving others, rarely in relation to our selves. In the short term, we experience a deep tiredness and a gradual reduction of energy and enthusiasm to deal with other people's needs, even if this is an integral part of our work. We tend not to put this into words because there is simply no context in which to describe these feelings: instead we end up feeling alternately resentful and guilty.

In the course of a lifetime, we refer to an awareness of something missing, an emptiness or restlessness, an inexplicable sadness, which originate from this unfulfilled need. The long-term effect is a drastic lowering of self-esteem, a loss of touch with the self, with an intrinsic source, causing a deep sorrow. Some seed, some possibility withers and dies and that grief lies deep in our hearts often without ever being named.

Once we recognise the need for separateness, we realise at the same time how much we have lost touch with this need. It is easy to get so caught up with our roles and responsibilities and our emotional connections with others that we lose sight of the fundamentally vital need to take time for ourselves. We end up over-loaded and unbalanced.

Losing sight of the need for separateness and self-nourishment affects our capacity to attend clearly to the requirements of others. Re-acquainting ourselves with the need to inhabit or revisit the space of our *own* being can help us take practical steps to meet this need when necessary and restore the balance. The very compassion that we rediscover for ourselves renews the desire for and facility for love, compassion and tenderness towards others.

Now we move on to the second polarity which may seem more unusual in its conception.

Engagement ←————————————→ Containment

The second polarity encompasses our needs to engage with others and to be contained by them. The need for engagement describes the need to be 'met', to be stretched, matched, encountered, the need to feel and experience our self through interaction with others. The need for containment describes the needs for finding the edges, the limits, the boundaries of that self through others. The first need pushes for self-expression, the second demands self-limitation, a firm structure within which to experience the restraining power of the other.

This is easily seen in childhood from the first 'No', to pushing against restraint and rules:

> 'Please can I?'
> 'Why can't I?'
> 'I will anyway, so there!'

Even before words are used, a baby will kick and struggle to find boundaries to test its physical power. And long into adolescence, the need to defy and exert power and identity emerges in the rebellious choice of dress, music, activities or friends. Yet this very struggle brings us to the opposite and essential need for containment. Teenagers need those very boundaries to kick against. This bruising period experienced by many parents is a clear example of how necessary it is to maintain restraint in order for the kicking to be felt.

The need for engagement is expressed in many ways throughout our lives: we need to get our teeth into things, to meet a challenge, and master it; we need to call others to account, to defy, to dare to change, to object, to call into question.

Experiences that meet our needs for engagement include:

Championing a cause
Fighting injustice
Breaking down barriers
Beating the system
Getting through the lights before they turn red
Passing an exam
Curing someone's illness
Making an impact
A heated debate

Taking the initiative
Scoring a goal
Overcoming limitations

The emotions in this polarity are based in *joy* and *anger*. When the need for engagement is fulfilled, through self-expression, overcoming an obstacle, breaking free from a restriction, the feelings are based in joy, ranging from elation, excitement and zest, to power, invincibility, celebration, pride and jubilation.

The complementary need is for containment. This is expressed through a need for structures around us within which to exercise our own will. To encounter an equal gives us the possibility of being fully who we are – to test our power in the confidence that the other will be there to resist. It is at the meeting point of our own boundaries and those of others that we can experience the source of true personal power.

We respond with similar emotions when our complementary need for containment is fulfilled. We can feel powerful, elated, dynamic and exuberant.

Experiences that meet our need for containment include:

Agreeing to disagree
Bowing to somebody else's will
Obeying
Honouring a contract
Putting someone else's needs first
Taking responsibility for ourselves
Accepting a refusal
Acknowledging our limitations
Knowing when to let go
Heeding the difference between persistence and useless
    perseverance
Giving in graciously

Experiences that block our need for engagement include:

Being bullied
Excessive criticism
Being a failure in a system
Being robbed
Not having the right qualifications or enough money

Being the victim of any kind of oppression
Being unfairly punished
Being cheated
Being crushed
Being unheard
Being ignored
Not being given a choice

When this need is blocked, the emotional response is based in *anger* with associated feelings of frustration, annoyance, irritation, fury, rage and indignation. When the complementary need for containment is inadequately met or neglected, again we feel anger, frustration, depression and despair.

Experiences that block our need for containment include:

Inconsistent rules and regulations
Random punishment
Being seen as an object
Someone 'moving the goal-posts'
Someone 'taking the rug out from under us'
Unclear boundaries
Dishonoured contracts
Someone breaking a hallowed tradition
Rape
Sexual harassment

When the need for engagement or the complementary need for containment are restricted or suffocated, our emotions are based in *anger*. It is essential to understand what is meant in this context by anger, because this is probably the most misunderstood of all the emotions. What we have become accustomed to call anger is not anger at all but a distorted expression of anger that emerges in the familiar form of *aggression*.

Aggression v. Anger

The complementary needs described earlier are for engagement and containment. At its most fundamental source, this polarity is embedded in a yearning for *equality*. It is only through an equal encounter that we can learn our true limits. A small human being will push towards self-assertion, needing to have that assertion contained through acknowledgement and recognition and encountering. When this 'push' is limited, restrained, refused in any way, this small human being will feel anger – a natural and healthy response to the obstruction of personal energy forwards and outwards – and express it somehow.

If the anger is released and met and matched, the child experiences containment, in other words, a boundary against which to stretch and develop and test his own limits. This is because it is vital to test our own will (engagement) but equally vital to recognise and accept another's greater power (containment). It is necessary to experience the limitations of our will, capacities and strength; to accept that there are times when we have to yield, and experience the regret and frustration that may accompany that acceptance.

When we experience, as children or adults, not being matched but oppressed, the outcome is different. There is no possibility of encounter when two *unequal* forces meet in opposition: the greater force will reduce the lesser, becoming more inflated, while the lesser force is diminished. In other words, instead of feeling held or contained by a boundary, we feel crushed by it and powerless. In that swamp of powerlessness breeds the virus of aggression. Aggression is a conditioned and learned response to the experience of inequality and oppression.

This confusion affects our attitude to the need for containment. The association of joy or contentment with gestures of obedience or acquiescence or surrender makes little sense in a world that interprets such behaviour as defeat, humiliation and a failure to win. And yet, it is a vital need, to feel that boundary of another in order to provide the security of knowing our limits and accepting them. This is not the same as learning one's position in the pecking order: it is learning how to negotiate power, how to exercise power without oppression.

Part of the difficulty we have in understanding the distinction between anger and aggression is that they have become so intertwined in our behaviour and attitudes that we believe them to be synonymous. But they are quite different, both in substance and in expression, as will become clear throughout the following chapters.

Now we come to the third and final polarity.

Safety ←————————————————————→ Risk

The need for safety encompasses the human need for recognition, repetition, routine, familiarity. It describes our need to know where we belong and to experience enough consistency around us to be able to structure our own sense of identity, to know who we are and where we are. The impulse is to understand, make sense of and to order the randomness of our environment. This is essential in order to be able to trust.

The safety born of this trust is vital for emotional and intellectual development. Very early on an infant will recognise the pattern of her mother's face and at around seven months will express fear at unfamiliar faces. An older child will be reluctant to leave those who are familiar to him and to go off with a stranger, however safe the stranger. Children often want to hear the same story over and over again because knowing the ending reinforces a sense of safety. Even more sophisticated adolescents will regress to childish hostilities precisely because they feel safe enough at home to release some of the anxiety and tension experienced when away.

At the opposite end of this polarity is the need for **risk.** The stimulus of uncertainty is essential if we are to expand or learn, or develop our knowledge and experience. There is a point when the familiar becomes stultifying and claustrophobic, when the known loses its stimulus, when routine becomes a rut. This is when we consciously or unconsciously realise that we need to shift the balance. We need to leave something or someone behind, make a change, confront our anxieties or take a gamble on something different and new.

Experiences that meet our need for safety include:

Making a home
Being able to be ourselves with others
Being understood
Being recognised with a smile
'Getting through' to someone
Familiar objects in our environment
A supportive arm around us when we are feeling vulnerable
Being part of a social/professional/peer group
Making it safe for someone to learn
Holding someone's hand when they are frightened
Gaining confidence in a new skill

Finding the right words
A favourite pair of slippers
Someone telling us the truth

The emotions in this final polarity are based in *trust* and *fear*.
When our need for safety is met we respond with feelings of relaxation, peace, trust, confidence, a sense of belonging and security, the
pleasure of being accepted, the joy of speaking the same language,
contentment and happiness.

The same range of feelings occurs in response to the fulfilment of
the complementary need for risk.

Experiences that meet our need for risk include:

Learning a new skill
Trying any new behaviour
Breaking from a stale relationship or job
Initiating a difficult conversation
Standing in the minority
Speaking out when we are not sure what we are going to say
Travelling to foreign lands
Going for a new image
Making the first move in a new relationship
Braving disapproval
Deciding to do something different for Christmas

What happens when our needs for safety or for risk are blocked?
The emotional base is fear, with feelings ranging from anxiety
through worry, panic, alarm and terror.

Experiences that block our need for safety include:

Being lied to
Being unable to find the right words
Living with someone's unpredictable moods
Awaiting the result of a biopsy
Being identified by the colour of our skin or the shape of our
    body
The threat of redundancy
Being powerless in the hands of 'experts'
Being alone and vulnerable
Worrying about paying the bills

Experiences that block our need for risk include:

Being over-protected
Being ridiculed for losing
Being called stupid
Over-dependence on the approval of others
Believing we have got to say the right words at the right time
The promotion of prejudice
Never having to take responsibility
The belief that there is only one right way
Allowing no room for mistakes

There are times when too much uncertainty indicates that a wiser course is to return to the safe and familiar for a while. There are times when we need to break out, to address our fears and take a risk. Again, it is the complementary need that often comes as more of a surprise. It is easier to associate anxiety and fear with lack of safety than lack of risk. In a conscious attempt to avoid fear, we often fail to take risks, we hide behind others, we don't dare to let go control or step beyond a known personal limit because of too much free-floating anxiety. As fear is seen culturally as a negative emotion, there is a constant discouragement from acknowledging or experiencing it. Instead we are encouraged to believe that elimination of risk in any experience is actually more desirable. The outcome, ironically, on an individual and collective level, is that instead of feeling more confident or safer, we actually become more anxious.

Understanding that emotions and feelings arise in healthy response to certain experiences helps us become more familiar with the rhythms of all three polarities. Managing the balance within each of them is an important aspect of emotional and mental health as we begin to see more clearly how they operate in our lives. Without information, we often find that emotions run riot in our lives, sometimes interfering with our ability to function in the way we want to.

Louise, as a young woman, found herself almost incapacitated by indecisiveness and worry. The slightest decision would fill her with panic and doubt about her ability to make the right choice. Her parents had lavished everything on her as a child, and this extended to continuous financial support as an adult. Loved as she undoubtedly was, she had never experienced the risk of managing for herself, proving herself capable of being independent. The longer this continued, the more afraid she became of ever being able to stand on her own feet because she had never experienced the balance between the needs for risk and safety. This fear seeped into every area of her life, destroying her trust in herself.

For Gavin, the problem was aggression. Quick-tempered by nature, he found it increasingly difficult to control his aggressive outbursts and was worried because he was becoming more violent. Like many men, his response to any feeling whatsoever was aggression, having learned as a boy not to admit to sadness or fear. Understanding the full range of his emotional responses set him on the road to monitoring and changing his behaviour.

To Dawn, the three polarities made sense from another perspective. For a year, she suffered from apathy and loss of real interest in her family or clients or any of the other people in her life. After thirty years devoted to the needs of others, she had withdrawn from

Figure 3   *The three polarities*

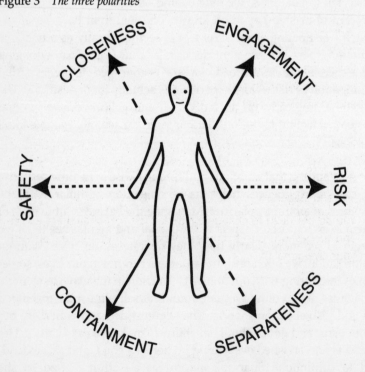

life without understanding why. Learning about the need for separateness, she realised that this was a need she had neglected for too long and was able to plan the future more positively to incorporate it into her life.

In order to relate the theory of these three polarities to our own lives, it helps to understand that the emotions of *love* and *grief*, *joy* and *anger*, *trust* and *fear* are *all* valuable, essential and intrinsic to human existence and development. I have separated them to explain the relevance of each but, of course, our experience is of all three polarities simultaneously, with one or other dominant at different times. Together, they form the raw material of the emotional capacities with which, alongside our biological, intellectual and spiritual capacities, we are born.

◆ Look again at the examples of the different polarities in this chapter. Take the past seven days of your life, and review them, quietly identifying at least two occasions, however small or ordinary, on which the needs for closeness, for engagement and for security were each met.

◆ Follow the instructions given above, but this time find two occasions on which your needs for separateness, for containment and for risk were met.

◆ Note whether the polarities feel balanced in your life, or whether it is difficult to find examples for one aspect of a polarity. If there is a difficulty, consider whether this is/has been a continuing difficulty throughout your life, or whether it is simply part of your current age and stage.

◆ You do not need to change anything. The aim of all these exercises and suggestions is to become more aware of the pushes/pulls in your emotional life.

---

3 | Heartscape

THE next step in applying the theory to the reality of our lives is to gain some understanding of how these emotional capacities have been affected by our experiences to date, leaving us with our present **heartscape** – our individual emotional make-up. The ultimate composition and complexity of each heartscape makes it as unique as a fingerprint. However, as with our physical make-up, we have structural features in common. We all have the capacity to be emotional as we have the capacity to be intellectual or spiritual but we differ in basic emotional disposition.

Consider your own emotional disposition: would you describe yourself as an emotional person or unemotional on the whole? Being emotional doesn't mean you have more emotions than average; being unemotional doesn't necessarily imply being heartless. I find it helpful to imagine our range of emotional disposition in relation to the structure of a coastline and the effect of emotional **'tides'**.

Twice a day, a swell of water sweeps around the coastlines that bound our oceans, powered by the gravitational pull of the sun and moon. The swell rises to one metre high, moving like the hand of a clock, but in an anti-clockwise direction, taking approximately twelve hours to complete its cycle. This is what we call a tide. As the 'hand' approaches a section of coastline, the water along the shore slowly rises to become a high tide. As the crest of the swell sweeps past and away, the tide falls. In this way, both high and low tides alternate every six hours or so, continuously, day and night.

For some individuals, 'tides' of emotion occur with similar regularity and frequency. These individuals, whom I call *coastliners*, inhabit the emotional coastline all their lives and are highly sensitive to changes in mood and current in themselves, in others and in their environment.

Other individuals, the *inlanders*, inhabit the inland psychic regions away from the immediacy of the ebbs and flows experienced along the coast. Their emotional rhythm is slower. More comfortable with their feet on solid ground than swimming in uncertain currents, they are nevertheless conscious of and responsive to the presence and influence of the ocean, even if it is not in direct view.

In our particular culture, a coastliner is more readily identified as being 'over-emotional', possibly 'sick' if her problems are blamed on her emotions rather than on her inability to understand and manage her emotions effectively. An inlander, in our culture, might regard himself as utterly stable and a model of rationality until his wife announces she wants to end their marriage after twenty years because she has grown tired of his 'distance' and lack of emotional warmth. Only then perhaps would he be shocked into considering his own emotional reality.

At times when the moon is at its fullest or darkest point, the normal swell and fall of the tide is intensified. Similarly, human emotions are intensified and diminished by cyclical changes. Some people experience regular emotional tides when influenced by cyclic hormonal changes, others are aware of emotion only in response to external disruption and changes in their lives, whether expected or unexpected, directly or indirectly experienced.

Learning about feelings helps us to avoid the dangers of imbalance at both extremes. Coastliners risk being swept out to sea and losing sight of land completely, struggling to stay afloat, floundering and sometimes drowning in depression and addiction. Inlanders risk becoming totally landlocked, losing touch with the heart entirely, stranded in an arid and toneless rigidity, suppressing any emotional manifestation in themselves and others.

Most individuals fall along a continuum, between the coastliners and inlanders, moving back and forth a little as circumstances change, but never far. Although long-term medication or drug abuse can alter our emotional disposition, it is unlikely that someone will stop being naturally more sensitive or less changeable. This basic disposition remains fairly constant even when we learn to explore our personal heartscape and to manage our own emotions more effectively.

What accounts for individual difference within the broader perspective? The formation of an individual heartscape will depend on many personal circumstances: the age or disposition of our parents, whether we have one or two carers, whether or not we have siblings, whether we were born male or female, and our position in the family. It will also be affected by impersonal factors: the age into which we are born and prevailing social trends.

In western culture, for example, fathers are now encouraged to take a more active role than they were fifty years ago; more marriages end in divorce and so more children experience being brought up by one parent. Fashions in breast-feeding, trends in approaches to education and discipline, the incidence of women working outside the home, times of social unrest or calm, boom or recession: all these factors contribute to our experience of childhood.

Let us suppose that a child comes into being not as a *tabula rasa*, nor entirely predetermined, but containing the potential for spiritual, intellectual, emotional and physical development and maturity. This potential will vary from child to child but, within each child, it will be shaped by experience so that it may be realised fully, partially or not at all.

Whether we remember our childhood as predominantly happy or sad, secure or insecure, our parents as close and loving or distant and unsupportive, every one of us experiences our needs being both met and unmet. Whatever happens to us, whatever the circumstance of our early environment, into whatever era we are born, one thing is guaranteed: we will experience emotions of many shades and intensities with differing names and emphases. Emotion will be a constant aspect of our childhood as it is for the rest of our lives.

From the earliest stages of life, a human being develops through the experience of constantly moving back and forth along the three basic polarities of existence. Movement allows us to learn, to unfold and to develop. Whatever the individual experience, there are common factors which make us especially susceptible, as children, to being affected by what happens to us.

The first of these factors is *vulnerability*. The absolute dependence of the infant makes him extremely vulnerable. Because there is no division between psyche and soma, physical needs are identical with psychological needs: being filled with good food *is* being filled with good love, whereas, later, as adults, being fed is *symbolic* of being cared for. The infant has no capacity for comprehension, no capacity for tolerance of need, and, at first, no capacity for differentiation between self and mother, between self and need. In the first weeks and months of infancy, any absence, physical deprivation or mistreatment will cause deeper and more permanent damage than it might do later on.

Two other major factors affect the long term influence of our experiences: intensity and frequency. *Intensity* refers to the quality of the stimulus – the depth, power and extent of its impact and its capacity to affect us. *Frequency* describes the number of times we experience the stimulus: obviously, the more often something occurs and is reinforced, the more the potential for arousal. This applies throughout childhood: the severity or satisfaction of an experience will be more deeply etched on our psyches simply because the wax is softer and more malleable and if the same lines are etched over and over again, through repetition of a particular experience, they create a furrow that is never erased.

The confluence of vulnerability, dependence, biological and intellectual immaturity is unique to infancy. Later in life, we may again feel vulnerable, we may again be dependent but, unlike the infant, we have an adult capacity to comprehend, to conceptualise, and physically we are more resistant to harm.

Figure 4   *A child's experience of the three polarities*

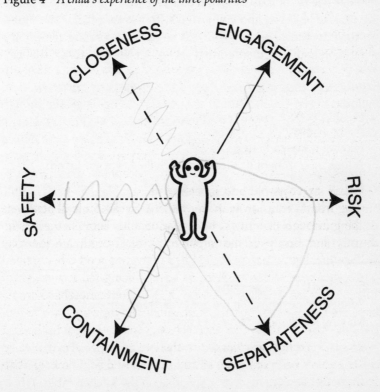

First, we will look at the kinds of experiences that meet or block our needs along the closeness/separateness, engagement/containment and safety/risk polarities. The examples will appear very similar to those in the previous chapter but their difference lies in the way they are experienced by a child. In infancy and childhood, being comforted or rejected, being punished or praised, have different implications.

It is simpler again to look at the three polarities in turn. This time, try to imagine how much 'larger than life' these experiences can be for a child, remembering how urgent our needs were then and how intensely we feel the response. The hallmarks of childhood responses are their simplicity and the huge significance of what is communicated without words.

Closeness ←————————————→ Separateness

Even without speech a child will develop the ability to communicate her needs for closeness and separateness. We learn to balance the wish to be loved and comforted with learning that, sometimes, we have to wait. Learning how to be alone, tolerating temporary separation knowing that reunion will occur, is part of this balance.

Experiences that meet our need for closeness as children include:

Being listened to
Having it kissed better
A look or comment or touch which tells us we are loved

Jack is six years old and is feeling vulnerable. His head is still hurting from a collision with the turnstile at the football stadium. Walking through the crowd, he is glad that his small hand is held warmly and firmly in the larger hand of his fourteen-year-old brother, Jim.

Someone taking a genuine interest in us
Being loved even when we get everything wrong
Making someone we love feel better

Emma, aged five, has worked really hard on a special card for her mother who's been unhappy since her granny died. She keeps the card a secret and leaves it as a surprise on the kitchen table. When her mother finds the card and opens it, the smile on her mother's face fills Emma heart with happiness.

Being praised and encouraged
Feeling we're special
Our parents being proud of us

Ben is nine. This year, in a school competition, his design for a T-shirt is selected to commemorate the annual school marathon. Every child in the school is wearing 'his' T-shirt on the day. His parents come to watch the event and Ben sees in their eyes how immensely proud they are of his achievement.

Experiences that meet our need for separateness as children include:

Doing homework in your own room
Having permission to be absorbed in your own world
Time away from the family spent with a favourite relative
Time to play, to fantasise and to invent our own rules

Space is extremely limited in seven-year-old Gary's house. There are five children, so no one has their own bedroom. Every now and then, when the weather is fine (and even when it isn't), he disappears to the bottom of the garden where he has cleared a space in a convenient hollow in the body of a large bush. With his parents' support, he is allowed to keep it as *his* space in which he can 'hide' and be alone when he needs to be.

Being able to go off and sulk knowing we can come back
Going for a bicycle ride
Being absorbed in reading a story
Our privacy being respected

Rebecca, aged eleven, sometimes surprises her parents by announcing she wants to go to bed early. She doesn't intend to sleep; she just wants to be quiet. There is so much going on in her life – her stepbrother's moods, her dislike of the new teacher, the plans for her uncle's wedding, the everyday ups and downs of her life – that it gives her an opportunity to think, sort things through and come back to herself on her own.

When the needs related to this polarity are fulfilled, we feel *love, contentment, happiness, pleasure, delight, warmth, peace.*

Experiences that block our need for closeness as children include:

Being mocked, belittled, humiliated
Unkind labels or nicknames that stick
Loss of a parent or sibling through death
Constant criticism
Loss of a familiar environment

Debbie is eight and her family has recently moved a long way from their previous home. Her parents are busy settling in; her elder brother is away at school. The children at her new school tease her because she speaks differently. She misses her best friend, Mandy, terribly and is feeling very lonely.

Being criticised for something we cannot change, e.g. physical
    appearance, physical or mental abilities
Physical, sexual, emotional cruelty or abuse
Excessive punishment
Lack of interest

David was seven when his father died and his mother's attitude towards him suddenly changed. She found it difficult to look at him or touch him because she felt immediately reminded of her lost husband. This meant that, just at the time he most needed his mother's love, she withdrew her affection from him.

Experiences that block our need for separateness as children include:

Over-possessiveness
Having to kiss or hug or participate when we don't want to
Lack of privacy
Inappropriate disclosure of parents' emotional problems and
    difficulties

While Brian's father is away, which is most of the time, his mother often pours out her sadness and frustrations. He is six and sensitive. He knows she is unhappy about his dad and he has seen her crying a lot since his baby sister was born. He tries his best to be her 'little man' but the weight of it all sits heavily on his small shoulders, interfering with his own needs to be separate from her.

Having to eat food when we don't want it
Too much emotional stimulation and demand
Lack of acceptance

Abbie really enjoyed playing an old piano in the garage, she would lose herself in the sounds and forget everything else for a while. One day, she came back from school to find the piano had gone: her parents had cleared it away, not realising how important it was to her. Even when she burst into tears, they found it hard to know what she was making such a fuss about.

When the needs related to this polarity are *blocked* in these ways, we feel *sadness, grief, loss, hurt, pain, loneliness, cold* and *emptiness*.

Now we turn to the second polarity. As with the previous one, the illustrations can be one-off incidents or patterns of experience which last for a short while or over many years.

Engagement ←————————→ Containment

Between engagement and containment, a child learns to exist in relation to others. She learns she has an identity, a name, that some things – belongings, abilities, her body, her parents – are hers and some things belong to others: the fundamental rubric of boundaries.

Experiences that meet our need for engagement as children include:

Being stretched and challenged, physically and mentally
Permission to express our feelings
Solving problems
Doing things ourselves

At the age of three, Kevin insisted on dressing himself on the day the family was going to visit his grandparents. Although his mother would have preferred that he hadn't got his clothes inside out and back to front, she lets him stay as he chooses, without correcting him.

Participation in tasks and discussions
Wrestling playfully with peers
Being useful
Being given responsibility

Toby is thrilled to be allowed to walk the neighbour's dog. He loves to exercise the necessary authority, to issue the appropriate instructions, while at the same time being mindful of safety and taking care when he meets other dogs.

Our parents being proud of who we are
Being effective
Having our 'No' accepted sometimes

Sally and her brother are doing their homework. He asks if she knows the capital of Australia. 'Sydney,' their dad butts in. 'No, it's not. It's Canberra,' Sally retorts. The argument continues until an encyclopaedia proves her dad wrong. 'I was right,' declares Sally. 'You were, love, well done,' replies her dad. She watches him just to check if he minds but his evident enjoyment at being challenged shows her there's no need to worry.

Competitive play
Being able to express anger without punishment
Our feelings, needs, opinions, decisions being considered
Being able to teach adults something

Shaheen is ten and hears her aunt complaining that she knows nothing about computers. Shaheen offers her a lesson which is eagerly accepted and she feels important and proud to be able to teach her.

Now we look at the complementary need for containment, a need of which, as adults, we are scarcely aware. Children are even less conscious of it, yet our developing self-esteem relies as much on this need being met as on the previous one.

Experiences that meet our need for containment as children include:

Learning the rules
Clear limits, consistently set
Being told 'No' when necessary

Darren, aged eight, is cross with his mother. He has spent too much of his pocket money on sweets and now he can't afford to buy a new video. She refuses to give or loan him any more because she insists he has to learn the value of money for himself. He has to accept that a 'No' sometimes means no.

Learning to respect authority
Experiencing anger as love
Fair and consistent punishment

Stuart is given detention after school for a whole week when he and his mates are caught smoking. He is annoyed because it means he will miss his football practice but he knows the rules even if he doesn't like them.

Learning to put someone else's needs before our own
Learning to share
Learning to see our parents as individuals

After endless quarrels and tantrums about the time she should be back home, Clare's mother asks her to sit down and listen. Her mother explains how much she worries when she is out late and, at the age of fourteen, Clare begins to understand what her mum goes through and that the fight is not about being treated like a child but more like being expected to behave as an adult.

When these needs are met the emotions include: *pride, joy, zest, vitality, hope* and feelings of *strength, force* and *dynamism*.

Experiences that block our need for engagement as children include:

Necessary or unnecessary restrictions on behaviour
Being told 'No!'
Exclusion from all decision-making
Having your talents/efforts continually belittled or discouraged

Ruth is constantly compared to her sisters, who, as she is often reminded, are pretty or intelligent or talented. If she gets praise at school or succeeds in a task at home, her parents respond with mute but unmistakeable disappointment. Her siblings have learned to cast her in the role of family dunce, a role that, as her sense of self dwindles to nothing, she accepts as she becomes excluded from real participation within the family.

Being told constantly, 'You can't', 'You're not good enough'
Being blamed for a parent's or sibling's unhappiness or failure
Being told constantly, 'Say you're sorry!'
Never being able to participate

Discouragement from challenging the status quo
Being subjected to outside rules and regulations
Excessive punishment
Invasion of physical/psychological boundaries by physical,
    sexual or emotional abuse
Being punished for spontaneous behaviour

It is Stephen's seventh birthday. He is bounding round with excitement in anticipation of his friends coming to tea. The doorbell rings and Stephen runs to the door to open it, sees his friend on the doorstep and shouts 'Have you brought me a present?'

His father, upstairs, overhears this question and while the children are coming into the house, he shouts: 'Stephen! Come up here!' Stephen's heart sinks at the tone of his father's voice and he goes up. 'How dare you be so rude! You don't *ask* people whether they've brought you a present! Go to your room immediately.'

'But, Dad... I didn't mean to...'

'Go to your room,' his father repeats.

'My friends are coming...' His father gets hold of Stephen's collar and pulls him towards his bedroom, muttering, 'You'll do as I say. . .'

'Frank,' Stephen's mother calls up from below. 'Don't be so hard on him,' she tries to reason, 'it's his birthday.'

' I don't care if it's his birthday. He's got to learn good manners,' her husband replies. She is so accustomed to his bullying that she gives up.

Downstairs, the atmosphere is uncomfortable and awkward as the other children wonder where Stephen is. Upstairs, Stephen listens to his friends, biting back his tears and his small heart hardens with bitterness and hatred.

Experiences that block our need for containment as children include:

Inconsistent rules
Never being given a clear and inflexible 'No!'
Never knowing the limits

Martin was a longed-for child. His parents found it hard to say no to him. He learned to push and push, knowing that he would always get his way in the end. This has happened all his short life. Normal boundaries – regarding bedtimes, homework, eating habits, spending money, acceptable and unacceptable behaviour – have always been weak. Martin's needs for something to fight *against* and yet be contained *by* have been unmet. He is now twelve, is as tall as his mother, and he has already started bullying and threatening her.

Never having to take responsibility
Over-protectiveness
Excessive severity of punishment
Inconsistent punishment

Katie is an only child. Her father is an unhappy man: his work, his wife, his whole life frustrate him. He is a little afraid of his wife's critical tongue and finds it easier to lash out at Katie when his feelings get the better of him. She never knows when this will be. She has no way of protecting herself from the shock of the violence except to withdraw more and more into her own world.

Learning only the roles of bully and victim
Learning that obedience is losing face
Being exploited
Being the butt for a parent's destructive behaviour

When our needs related to this polarity are blocked, we feel *anger, frustration, rage, hatred, powerlessness, depression, disappointment* and *despair.*

Now we look, in the same way, at the final polarity.

Safety ←——————————————→ Risk

Between safety and risk, a child can acquire a sense of public and private; a sense of the interior and exterior aspects of self. This involves balancing a realisation that some thoughts we can talk about, some things we share only with those we trust and other thoughts we keep to ourself.

Experiences that meet our need for safety as children include:

Being talked to, not at
Enough consistency and routine
Being taken seriously even when we can't put it into words

Someone to hide behind when we are afraid
Learning to make yourself understood in gestures and words
Being included
A comforting object to stroke or suck
Truthful answers to our questions

Sara's mother had been ill for a while now and was getting thinner and thinner. Sara had carried round a knot of fear inside her for ages and felt sick but nobody would say anything, even when she asked what was happening. Finally, when they were alone, she plucked up the courage to ask her mother if she was going to die. Her mother looked at her in silence for a few seconds and then replied: 'Yes, I am going to die, Sara. It's time for us to talk, isn't it?'

Being able to be oneself
Making sense of others
Our difference being accepted
Someone understanding what we are trying to say
A worn teddy bear
Promises being kept

Jamie's parents are divorced so he doesn't get to see his father often. On the last occasion, several weeks ago, his dad had promised him a new bicycle for his eighth birthday. Jamie is very nervous as he waits for his dad to pick him up. Would he remember what he'd promised? Would he have forgotten because he didn't see him much any more? Did his dad still love him?

The car draws up. Jamie watches his dad through the window. He sees him get out of the car with a large parcel. He opens the door: the grin on his dad's face and the shape of the parcel tell him that the promise has been kept.

Experiences that meet our need for risk as children include:

Being given confidence to make decisions
Being encouraged to trust our instincts
Being congratulated on having taken a risk
Encouragement to imagine and to play
Encouragement to have a go regardless of the outcome

Michelle didn't want to go camping with the Brownies for a week. She was nine and had never stayed away from home that long before. She got herself into a dreadful state with worry and nerves. Her parents listened to her fears sympathetically but encouraged her to go, reminding her she could phone every evening and, if it was really dreadful, they would come and fetch her.

The first night she phoned, in tears, saying it was awful. They suggested trying one more day. The second night she sounded much happier. She didn't bother to ring again because she was having such a good time.

A patient presence while we try to do it for ourselves
Someone holding the bicycle when we ride for the first time
Learning a new skill
Encouragement to explore and to find out our own answers
It being acceptable that we don't know the answer
It being all right when we get it wrong

Anna was mortified. She had forgotten some of her lines in the play and she knew her parents had been out there somewhere, watching her make a fool of herself. She looked for them anxiously in the crowd of people leaving the school and then she saw them. They saw her at the same time and she ran to them, saying how sorry she was. But she didn't need to apologise. Her mum gave her a huge hug and said she'd been so brave to stand up there and her mistake hardly showed; her dad said it was the best evening out he'd had in ages and that they were all going out to celebrate.

When our needs relating to this polarity are met, we feel *trust, fearlessness, confidence, relaxation, belonging, security, excitement.*

Experiences that block our need for safety include:

Denial
Dishonesty
Broken promises
Being called stupid for feeling afraid

Thomas is four and his family is on holiday by the sea. His father was brought up by the sea and is determined that Thomas should get used to the water. Thomas doesn't like the water. He doesn't want to swim. He is frightened. His father tells him not to be silly, there's nothing to be afraid of, picks him up and wades into the water. Thomas screams and struggles.

Thomas's fear increases. His struggle to get away now turns into a desperate fight to hang on to his father, he begs him not to let go. His father throws him in: the shock, the water in his nose and throat, the pounding in his ears, the sheer terror of it all overwhelm him. He gasps for air and flays his arms around, glimpsing his father standing there, convinced he's done the right thing for his son.

Sudden or unexplained presence or absence
Deceit and pretence
Threats of abandonment
Living in constant fear of punishment or abuse

Tracey is nine. She is in bed in the middle of the night. She is terrified because she can hear her eighteen-year-old stepbrother making his way up the stairs towards her room. She knows he will creep in; that he will not speak; that he will lift up the duvet and lift up her nightie; that he will start stroking between her legs and put his fingers into her. She knows that he will lie on top of her heavily and squash her, putting his penis where his fingers have been and that it will hurt so she has to try and blank out and keep quiet. She knows that if she makes a sound he will put his sweaty, sticky hand over her mouth. She knows she will pray for him to get to the juddering bit quickly so it will be over. She tells nobody. She is afraid to because he told her once never to mention it. He is her mother's only son.

Random punishment or violence
Our private confidences discussed in public
Unpredictable emotional absence of parent through depres-
    sion, alcoholism, drugs, etc.

As soon as he hears his dad coming home, Simon's whole body stiffens with tension. He never knows what his dad's mood will be. Sometimes when he's been drinking, he'll come home happy and other times, he'll be mean and nasty to everyone; sometimes he starts off being nice but then he changes suddenly. Simon can never relax.

Experiences that block our need for risk as children include:

Absence of mental stimulation
Lack of acceptance of mistakes or clumsiness
Over-emphasis on the dangers of failure/looking foolish etc.
Being over-protected

Helen is keen to go on the school skiing trip with the rest of her friends. Her father has never skied before and considers it a dangerous sport. Her mother has a dreadful head for heights and tends anyway to live her life on the safe side. They keep telling her that she could easily be injured, if not even killed. As they are so concerned about her safety, they think it best for her not to go.

Discouragement from creative expression
Having always to get it right
Having always to say something 'intelligent'
Criticism for making mistakes

Peter hates French. His teacher is a stern man who is excessively severe when it comes to mistakes. Only the really good pupils speak up, because if you make an attempt and get it wrong, he mimics you in an unkind way. Peter has tried but he doesn't want to look silly in front of everyone again so he no longer speaks up. He dreads it being his turn to answer a question and his anxiety makes it impossible to learn anything at all.

Being told there is only *one* right way
Being brainwashed into believing we're non-achievers
Being taught to disregard intuition

In response to these experiences, we feel *anxiety, worry, nervousness, tension, fear, terror, intimidation, dread.*

It is useful to separate out the three polarities and their major emotions, in order to understand where our feelings come from but, as we saw in Chapter 2, our actual human experience of emotion is of course a *combination* of threads involving all three polarities. Reading through the examples of children's experiences, it is easy to see that there will be a mixture of feelings involved. The child who is loved and able to give love will feel more trusting and confident and be able to live with more energy and spontaneity. When a child is treated with contempt or without affection, the accompanying feelings automatically diminish his capacity to trust, inhibit confidence and the ability to risk, and restricts his sense of power and self-esteem.

You will probably have found at least a few examples with which you are familiar from your own experience as a child, and perhaps as a parent. With the best parental will in the world, all of us, as children, are subject to a mixture of fulfilment and interruption of our needs. What matters is not what happens or when, or whether our parents could have done a better job of parenting; the most important aspect here for gaining insight into our personal heartscapes is *to understand how we dealt with the emotions that arose* in response to whatever we experienced. This is how the raw material of our being becomes fashioned into what we are and who we become throughout our lives.

◆ Take the time to make a retrospective journey now. You might like to make a simple drawing of yourself and the significant others in your life – parents, siblings, grandparents, relations, teachers – etc. and then add randomly what you remember as significant events. Are there single elements that you remember or general trends of parental influence, school days and so on? You are probably familiar with a lot of what you will include, but always be prepared for the element of surprise. Wait for things to come to you rather than writing down the obvious.

◆ When your drawing is complete enough, read again the section of examples of how the needs relating to the closeness/separateness polarity can be blocked or met, and note any that apply to your experience.

◆ Do the above for the engagement/containment polarity.

◆ Do the above for the safety/risk polarity.

---

4 | Processing emotion in our early years

THE examples of children's experiences in the previous chapter give an idea of the tenderness of our psyches when we're little and how deeply we depend on those around us. This is both normal and natural. Equally normal and natural is an inborn will to survive. To help us survive, we possess a vital facility: the capacity for psychosomatic (mind/body) release. During this time of extreme vulnerability, this capacity is intact.

An infant's responses to hunger, cold or pain (unfulfilled needs for food, warmth and comfort) are expressed spontaneously, immediately, fully, with accompanying screams, howls, cries, tears, sobbing, shaking, shivering, kicking. Release is automatic and uninhibited. There is no room yet for intervening self-conscious thoughts. It is surprising sometimes to witness the intensity of the rage and grief that emerge from such a tiny being, but it illustrates wonderfully our innate capacity for natural and spontaneous release. This signals psychosomatic distress to our carers, prompting them to feed, to hold, to rescue, to comfort and to restore the psychosomatic *balance*.

The modifications and restrictions of this vital capacity for emotional expression and release in any individual child's experience will set the foundation for adult emotional development. First, we look at what happens to this capacity before we learn to speak.

Pre-verbal experience

Any interruption or fulfilment, satisfaction or interference of our needs will arouse emotion more immediately and more intensely with a more permanent effect on our development than in later years.

Fulfilment – being loved, held, fed – assumes the proportions of all-encompassing bliss. Unmet needs – loss, pain, irritation, abandonment – assume the potency of a threat to existence. Our emotions in response to unmet needs therefore take on an extreme and exaggerated form: anger can be experienced as too powerful and dangerous, grief as too painful and fear as all-consuming. Each in its own way jeopardises our psychological and physical survival.

The combination of powerful emotions experienced in a tiny body generates extreme fantasies of loss, confusion, abandonment or destruction, any of which can threaten psychic survival. The defence-less infant needs above all to survive. Since survival is paramount, the psychosomatic mechanism sometimes shuts down as protection. This is known as *repression*. Stored in our memories are the experi-ences of such emotions, recorded in a raw, pristine state and likely to remain inaccessible so we can never truly make sense of them.

These memories carry a pre-verbal power, and as words are so useful in sorting out and refining emotions, we have less access to them. Therefore, the potency of these early emotions remains undi-minished. Unconscious primal images, memories, fears and fan-tasies remain in the fabric of our psyches, interwoven into normal adult emotional experience.

Sometimes these are detectable in the deeper, often inarticulable reaches of the human psyche. We touch them in our extremes of emotion: the physical and psychological magnetic power of erotic experience; the compelling need to curl up in and to lose ourselves in another; the fathomless depths of loss and isolation; the dread of disappearing altogether into tiny fragments; the deep-rooted horror of being smothered in relationship; the imagined devastating con-sequences of expressing anger.

Repression is a long-term control we unconsciously use to alter ideas and perceptions of an event, thus allowing us to 'forget' not only what happens but also our emotional responses to it because the arousal is intolerably painful at the time. This is part of an inbuilt safety mechanism which operates in the following way: whenever we are under dire threat, whenever our lives are in danger or we imagine them to be, whenever our energies have be focused on sheer survival, our emotional responses to what is happening are suspended. Our responses – our capacity for expres-sion and release – remain suspended until, if ever, we feel safe enough, until the danger has been averted, the threat is over, until survival is assured: then, and only then will our bodies allow us to feel the feelings involved. This mechanism operates throughout our lives (we will look at examples in Chapter 7).

In infancy, the 'suspension' becomes more or less permanent. The repressive mechanism functions like a massive door preventing access to what lies behind it. The emotions experienced in the past, but repressed, can be stirred into movement by triggers in the present but we will not be able to connect them consciously to the past. We all experience this to some extent and most of us suffer no impairment as a consequence. For a few individuals, however, the combination of vulnerability and severe, repeated trauma in very early life can lead to permanent intrusion in and confusion with external reality and recurring mental illness.

Our early years

Most of us, as infants, will experience enough of our needs being met. Most of us will be able to release our feelings through the physical mechanism available to us. The normal adult protective instinct towards a tiny child will ensure a degree of tolerance of tears and screams and yells. In infancy and very early childhood, the progression from response to arousal through maximum pressure to release and resolution is clearly visible.

I remember massaging Freya who was three years old. She was lying utterly content on her stomach while I massaged her small back for twenty minutes or so. When I had finished and took away my hands quite gently, her response was immediate: her ribs started to contract in deep sobbing. She got up and ran to her mother and cried for a minute or so in her mother's arms. Then it was over and forgotten. It struck me as a beautiful illustration of the human response to endings – sadness, loss and tears – the psychosomatic release simple, uncluttered and clear, and because she felt safe, the whole cycle was complete in a matter of minutes.

Completion of a cycle is signified by the ability to go on to something else. It can be seen in the way in which young children are able to feel rage or sorrow or fear so intensely in response to a refusal or a broken toy or a sudden tumble and a short while later, after the cycle of release is over, they have almost forgotten the incident. We have a short attention span. We are interested in immediate concerns and people and what matters is *now* rather than before or later. A child's perception of any stimulus will necessarily reflect his or her immature capacity for understanding the complexities of reality.

Jenny, aged five, was dressed up in a wonderful clown's outfit for the Hallowe'en celebrations with her friends in the neighbourhood. She was bubbling with excitement and delight at herself until she suddenly caught sight of another little girl dressed as a beautiful fairy. That was it! Sobbing inconsolably, her dreams in tatters, she was unable to understand that her mother could not immediately provide a similar fairy outfit for *her*. Her disappointment was immoderate, intense and immediate.

Any child needs safety to release his feelings. Joe, aged seven, for example, had developed quite a noticeable stammer and his older sister and parents would sometimes tease him affectionately by imitating his attempts to get his words out. On one occasion the teasing imitation started up again, but this time Joe suddenly exploded with anger, shouting 'Stop laughing at me' with a vehemence that took the rest of his family by surprise. But they took heed. His expression of anger informed them that the teasing had gone too far and enabled them to be more sensitive. The security he felt within his family enabled Joe to express and release his feelings.

This is not always the case. For many of us, as our independence increases, our emotional distress calls are seen as less acceptable, less necessary. While a young child will be comforted when crying after a sudden fall, in response to the shock and pain, an older child will be encouraged to be brave and hide distress and show more control. A cry of distress can be an uncomfortable unconscious reminder to adults of the dependence, vulnerability and all the feelings they themselves had to suppress as part of 'growing up'.

With developing consciousness, we learn to suppress our emotions. *Suppression* is a psychological mechanism that we use consciously to control our emotional responses in the short-term. This is a necessary skill but, as we will see, one that has become so over-used and automatic that it risks being more appropriately described as emotional *oppression*.

Learning to suppress our feelings doesn't stop us having feelings: it simply adds to the intensity with which we feel them. The vulnerability of our early years, as we have already seen, makes us more impressionable and susceptible to this intensity. In addition, we do not have the conceptual capacity to understand the total picture. What we feel is what we feel. As a child, we see things in black and white with no shades of ambivalence or subtlety. We see ourselves as the centre of the universe. If things go well, our parents are pleased; they love us and all is fine. If things go badly, our parents are displeased; if they reject us, our world collapses. This sensitivity and naivety continue throughout our childhood years. For this reason we need guidance if we are to make sense of our emotions and to *process* them sufficiently as they arise in response to our experience.

Our childhood needs are not always met. For all sorts of reasons, we will want food without getting it, we will want touch but have to do without, we will be frightened by things, we will encounter all sorts of restrictions, often for our own good. Emotional learning is integral to other learning. Sonia is told not to play with matches but because she *wants* to, she may be angry at this restriction – a natural response. If the anger is punished Sonia will learn that playing with matches is wrong and then, in addition, that spontaneous expression of *anger is wrong*.

When four-year-old Christopher's mother leaves the room and he is alone with another adult he doesn't feel comfortable with, he may well cry to bring his mother back. If he says to his mother he is frightened and, although she doesn't understand why, she is happy to comfort him, he will learn that his *fear is acceptable*. If he is scolded for being silly and babyish, and left uncomforted, he will learn the reverse.

Emotional education is a process of constant reinforcement through direct instruction and indirect absorption through hundreds of images, sensations, associations and memories.

Direct instruction

Much of our learning about emotional expression in childhood comes under the explicit and implicit all-embracing lesson of 'Don't!'

'Stop that noise.'
'Don't use that tone of voice with me.'
'Don't be such a baby.'
'We'll have none of your lip.'
'Stop blubbering.'
'Go upstairs until you can come down with a smile on your face.'
'Don't be silly.'
'There's nothing to be afraid of.'

'How dare you speak to me like that.'
'You're a big boy now.'
'Be a nice girl.'
'Be grown up.'
'Now, that's more like it.'
'If you don't stop crying, I'll give you something to cry about!'

and so on, with alternatives of reward or punishment to reinforce the desired behaviour. This includes subtle and non-verbal reinforcement: a raised eyebrow, the meaningful or menacing look, the cold shoulder, a smile of approval.

Indirect absorption

A fundamental method of teaching is through imitation and example. As children we are sensitive to atmosphere, to the presence of all emotions and even though we do not have the capacity to comprehend or to analyse or to articulate, we 'pick up' what is going on around us. We feel tension, we sense sorrow or rage or fear and because we see adults denying these feelings, hiding them, pretending otherwise, struggling to bite back or swallow back what they're feeling, we learn to do exactly the same.

Clearly, as children we are unable to balance emotion with insight and the perspective of experience. So we need guidance and help along the way to learn the vital lessons about emotion in the same way we learned vital lessons about other important aspects of life.

What was our experience as children? Was there an adult on hand to hold us and help us make sense of our feelings? Were we able to learn that release of emotion is acceptable but inappropriate in certain settings and better in the privacy of one's own home? Were we able to learn that emotions can be in response to things we imagine wrongly: that an absence or disappearance doesn't mean abandonment, or that someone's remark or gesture was not what we assumed but something different? Did we learn from a wise adult that someone else's unhappiness or anger can happen through no fault of our own but because of something inside *them*? Did we learn from a caring adult that strong, even loud and frighteningly intense feelings can be expressed without hurting or destroying anyone or anything else?

Did we learn that feelings were as seriously regarded as opinions? Did we discover the nuances of shade in feelings as we discovered nuances of colour in other parts of our lives? Did we have an adult on hand to help us make sense of our feelings especially when they were overwhelming, helping us to learn how to identify and manage and express our feelings as a normal part of growing up?

Did we learn that women cry more than men or that men shout more than women? Did we witness emotional expression used manipulatively: as a weapon to intimidate, to frighten, to coerce, to induce guilt or to achieve a particular goal? Did we learn, as with the tools of any other trade, that emotional expression can be used in particular ways: that the expression of one feeling will bring a smile to a parent's face whereas another elicits strong disapproval?

What we absorb during these early stages sets the foundation for the main period of learning about emotional communication and release. The first seven years or so are crucial, when we are old enough to think and yet still young enough to be instinctual. It is this 'subliminal' learning that affects us so deeply as children.

If we see from adult behaviour that feelings can be aroused, expressed, released, forgotten and genuine tranquillity restored, we learn that even though emotion can be frightening in intensity and suddenness, it will not last and it is not dangerous. If we see tears and rage escalating into terrifying cycles of aggression and violence which end in those we love, or ourselves, being badly damaged in the process, we learn that emotions arise as signals of danger.

What we learn by instruction and example will sow the seeds of our own emotional development or lack of it. This learning occurs through our interaction with the external environment. In the same way that, as children, we learn any language easily and permanently, so too we learn to speak the language of emotion or we learn to be silent. Of equal and parallel importance is what occurs *inside* our heads, our hearts and the rest of our bodies during these years.

To understand why our emotional learning differs from other types of learning, we have to remember the somatic aspect. We have to take into account the innate mind–body connection. This means that the memories of our experiences lie not only within our minds but also within our bodies. To understand fully how our behaviour is affected, we have to go beyond the cognitive level.

◆ Read the questions on pages 48–9 again and answer them from your own experience.

◆ Can you add additional emotional learning? What kind of picture do you build up in relation to the communication and release of emotions?

5 | Sequence: emergence and arousal

IN order to understand the psychosomatic (mind–body) connection, we need some idea of the process of emotional response. The physiology of emotion has long intrigued scientists who have explored this process in research laboratories. They have identified a three-part sequence: first, an event or stimulus; second, the interpretation and evaluation of that stimulus; and, third, our response in the light of this interpretation, which will be based on our past experience. This response is measured in terms of physiological arousal, and these physiological events are categorised as particular emotions.

This logical sequence makes logical sense, but in the laboratory both investigators and subjects are part of a simulated situation designed to examine a specific and isolated aspect of emotional–physiological response. This is very different from real-life experience where we are subject to random, sudden, perhaps overwhelming feelings that appear to come from nowhere. The emergence of emotions is often beyond our conscious control which is why being ambushed by feelings is a common experience.

If we understand that emotions are a constant potential within each of us we can begin to understand the importance of **perception.**

How we interpret what we hear and what we see, and how we respond as a consequence, will be affected by numerous factors: personal, psychological, physiological and situational circumstances, cultural expectations and the influence of past experience in the form of conscious and unconscious associations. The process of perception is extremely complex, which is why we can never assert with absolute authority that what we perceive, and therefore feel in response, is right.

A group of people can see and hear the same event but each person will respond differently according to his/her personal perceptions. Imagine, for example, the variety of possible responses among individuals in an audience at a concert. Perceptions will be influenced first by habitual or long-term factors: familiarity, taste, and musical knowledge. For example, someone might respond emotionally to the music without knowing a flute from a trombone; another might be predisposed to enjoy what she is hearing because the conductor is good-looking. Short-term factors influence our perceptions as well: one individual may be enjoying the rare treat of a night out and intent on enjoying herself regardless of the music; another could be anxious about impressing his new girlfriend; another's perception may be affected by a major row in the car on the way to the concert. Someone else may have seen in the audience a colleague he would prefer to avoid. A man who is proud because his son is playing in the concert and a woman who has worked hard to organise the whole event would again perceive and respond to the same concert quite differently.

A second important aspect of perception is that it is altered and intensified by *arousal*. An ingenious feedback system operates, involving the indivisible and constant interaction between mind and body. It works like the process of sexual arousal, which is another similar example of psyche and soma being indivisible. The more sexually aroused the person becomes, the more she/he perceives images and sensation as being arousing; this increases the body's state of arousal, which, in turn, increases the mental capacity to perceive stimuli as sexually arousing.

Emotional arousal works in the same way. A stimulus triggers a perception that elicits an emotion. When we are feeling sad and raw, we are more open to being affected by sad stories or sad music, and less able to hold back the flow of tears. It is a common experience that when we are feeling loved and delighted with ourselves, we are likely to regard others from an open-hearted and glowing perspective. It works in the other direction as well. During those tender weeks after a major bereavement, we can find ourselves hypersensitive to the potential for death and loss and grief everywhere around us which adds to the weight of our own sorrow.

The more angry we become, the more likely we are to perceive comments as infuriating and provocative, which then increases the anger. Imagine driving along a narrow country road to an important appointment, you are late and in a hurry. You find yourself behind a slow-moving car driven by an elderly lady. Yesterday you might have perceived her as endearing, but now she becomes in your mind an obstacle, a nuisance who clearly doesn't know how to drive and ought not to be doing so. Physically, your shoulders, neck, arms, spine and jaw will tighten, and as the prospect of arriving late looms larger, the psychosomatic arousal escalates into aggression: you start an internal monologue to wind yourself up – now she is deliberately driving slowly just to annoy you. This can escalate into all kinds of dangerous and risky manoeuvres on the road because your perception is distorted by rising fury. Alternatively, you might simmer all the way to your destination and vent your exasperation with a string of expletives after you get out of the car.

Once anxiety and fear take hold, we are likely to perceive more situations as fearful, which will in turn increase our fear. Walking home alone on a dark evening you hear footsteps behind you. Indistinct but frightening images, words of warning, rush through your mind, increasing the arousal of fear. Your body responds to your quickening heart-rate, your footsteps increase their pace, you look ahead to see how far you have to go to reach safety. Your body decides to run, mental and physical tension are focused on reaching home. You arrive and from the doorway you look out, see nobody, go inside and shut the door. Then you may release the fear a little with trembling or seek the comfort of something to steady yourself; if someone is there you may release more tension in a rush of words.

It is *essential* to understand that whether an emotion is minor or major, it always involves a process of change both in our **minds** (memories, associations, images, thoughts) and in our **bodies** (in blood pressure, muscle tension, skin and nerve receptors, heart-rate). The interplay between psyche and soma (mind and body) is **constant**.

Emotional arousal in an adult does not follow a simple curve from a low to a high point where the pressure demands release. There can sometimes be periods of quiescence, where the arc dips for a while before rising again, along a gradual or steep curve.

Once more, it is useful to compare this to the process of sexual arousal. A stimulus, sexual or non-sexual, physical or psychological, initiates the process. You can become aware that you feel turned on by a specific person or more generally feel sexually aroused with no particular person in mind. Sometimes it takes until the higher stages of arousal for us to realise that the process is under way. Once we are aware, choice and circumstance will dictate what happens next.

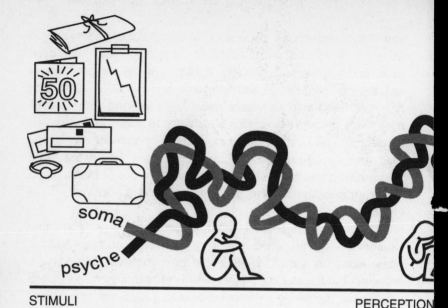

soma

psyche

STIMULI

PERCEPTION

Figure 5 *Emotional arousal*

If it is the wrong time or place, or you don't feel in the mood for whatever reason, it may go no further and dissipate. Should you decide to focus and pursue your desire, your body will tend to follow a pattern of response as the level of sexual arousal increases.

When an emotion is excited, the energy gathers momentum; there is a build-up of both physiological and psychological tension and pressure. The rate of emotional arousal will vary from individual to individual. There are long-term factors such as variations of temperament: we speak of someone having a short fuse and another person being slow to rouse to anger: we also refer to some people being over-sensitive whereas others are naturally thicker-skinned.

There are variations, too, which depend on the vulnerability of the individual. In other words, our potential to be affected by and aroused by what we perceive varies because we are more open and vulnerable at some times than others.

Vulnerability describes the state of being receptive and sensitive to the stimuli around us. In adults this generally tends to heighten at times of change when we are more open. Change can come in the form of a major life event: a death, a divorce, a new school, retirement. Times of change also include periodic cycles of hormonal levels that make us more sensitive to emotional arousal. Changes in

FEELINGS   TIME

scenery and in weather can affect our vulnerability. Extreme mental
or physical tiredness also increase our susceptibility because our
more rational defences are less resistant. So the aftermath of surgery,
a prolonged period of tension or the end of a busy term, can all
leave an individual emotionally more vulnerable.

The nature and purpose of emotion

To understand emotional arousal, we need to reconsider the nature
and purpose of emotion. It is an energetic impulse that passes
through us, like a wave, swelling to a peak at which it will then fall
and diminish. Emotion indicates our state of balance or imbalance
along the polarities. When our needs are met, we experience the
emotions of love, joy and trust, because we are in balance. When our
needs are obstructed or unmet, we experience emotions of grief,
anger and fear. It is these latter emotions that indicate that our needs
are not met: that something needs to happen so that the resulting
imbalance can be corrected. That 'something' can either be directly
meeting the need or an adequate release of the psychosomatic
tension that has been aroused. The two examples given earlier help
to illustrate this.

Walking alone at night, rising anxiety is a warning, informing us
to be alert, to seek protection and safety because there is danger.

Once we are safe – once we have met the need for safety – the balance is restored. Some of the chemicals aroused will have been used up in the effort to reach safety: excess chemicals can be released once safety is reached.

The arousal of frustration and anger when your progress is impeded by a slow driver illustrates another possible sequence. The efforts to rid ourselves of the obstruction will use up some of the aroused emotion and the build-up is likely to fall once we have arrived at our destination. However, we could still be aware of residual arousal which may dissipate slowly or quickly depending on circumstances.

In the process of sexual arousal, the accumulation of muscular tension, the combined effects of increased heart-rate, blood supply, heightened sensitivity of the nerve endings will build to a point where release is automatic. The tension, like air in a tyre, reaches bursting point: orgasm is a reflex response. The contractions of the muscles as the tension is dispersed will be experienced as strong or mild depending on how aroused you are and how much tension has accumulated. It can last a few seconds or spread spasmodically over a few minutes. The release can be felt as complete or partial. In other words, if the level of release matches the level of arousal, the experience is satisfying; when the level of release is lower than the level of arousal, the release is experienced as partial.

In the process of emotional arousal, a similar breaking point occurs. If we are aware of the rising emotional tension, we may continue to keep the hatches battened down. But at some point, our psychosomatic system has to give way: we reach the limit of mental and physical tolerance. There comes a point in the cycle of emotional arousal when no further tension can be tolerated and *release* of some sort becomes a natural and inevitable consequence.

Release is psychosomatic because emotion is a psychosomatic experience. It is a release both of bodily tension overload and mental tension overload. Just as the subjective experience of orgasm is difficult to put into words, because it occurs at a level ungoverned by rational or articulable thought, so, too, is the experience of emotional release.

Release into orgasm requires the person to 'disappear', to lose rational consciousness temporarily in order to yield to the physical experience. Authentic release of emotion also requires us to allow our bodies to follow a natural process without struggling against it.

Because there is generally so little understanding and so much fear and confusion about this process, it is important to look at the actual *inside* experience of emotional release.

◆ To locate emotion – where it belongs – in the body, take the time to see if you can recognise the physical signs of emotional arousal in your own body. In which muscles do you feel tension? What sensations are you aware of?

◆ Can you identify different emotions from the physical cues in your body? In other words, how does sadness feel different from frustration or anxiety? You may not be able to tell the difference at first, but list the physical sensations you are aware of.

---

6 | Sequence: release and resolution

RELEASE is easier to understand if we look at the polarities in turn because each of the three primary emotions is released differently.

Closeness ⟵————————————⟶ Separateness

The texture and release of grief. Some of the bodily clues which signal the arousal of emotion along this polarity are: smarting/prickling/burning/aching behind the eyes; tears welling up in the eyes; lump in the throat; difficulty in swallowing; nose running. Such signals tell us that feelings of sadness, hurt, longing, love, grief, happiness are aroused to some degree in us. If the arousal continues, these sensations will increase. The mind–body interplay will increase the intensity of these feelings in psyche and soma, so that the tension increases. The tension will ride out on the wave as it forms and tears will usually fall more profusely.

The release related to this polarity has its own pattern. If grief is allowed to be processed, the release will gradually work its way down from the chest, which will heave convulsively as tension is dispersed, towards the sternum, the upper abdomen, and then the lower abdomen which, in turn, deepen their contractions and the crying becomes sobbing, the rhythm becomes slower, the contractions between breaths becomes deeper. In its natural progression, the body will automatically bend forward with these deeper, low abdominal contractions, and often when very profound grief is being released the person will move spontaneously into a rocking motion back and forth.

Part of any natural release is sound. Natural sounds automatically relax the body, whereas completely silent activity indicates a holding in against the process and increases muscular tension. Release of sorrow and grief is often accompanied by sounds of grunting, groaning, small sounds at first, which if not restricted will naturally progress into deeper sounds which we associate with expressing physical pain: a groan, a low moan, eventually a low wail which seems to emerge from the depths of the psyche. To an observer, this can be heart-rending in its pitch and cadence, but it is essential for the individual to allow profound grief for death and separation and loss to be released fully.

The rhythm of release of feelings associated with this polarity is an even one with smooth undulations, varying considerably in depth but always naturally gentle rather than sharp, curved rather than linear, and like all authentic release, it has a natural rise and fall, a crescendo and diminuendo, an ebb and flow, a beginning and an end – if permitted.

Engagement ⟵⟶ Containment

The texture and release of anger. The words we use to describe some of the feelings related to this polarity give us clues to the arousal of the emotion of anger: restless, irritated, stifled, blocked, steaming, incandescent, explosive.

Heat is often experienced in the head, in the face, perhaps throughout the entire body. The energy is high, propelling us to act forcefully, to push, to exert strength against someone or something. As we struggle to restrain and contain this energy, the tension in the muscles increases: the jaw tightens, the muscles along the arms tighten, our fists clench, the buttocks, the thighs and the calves tighten; the heart quickens, the pulse increases.

The release of anger involves large movements; expansive, wide-reaching, moving away from one's self towards an external barrier. We are moved to punch cushions, stamp our feet, hit desks, throw objects, kick things, bang doors; when release is unmanaged, it can extend to hitting out indiscriminately at people. The need is for *impact*. Sound again is an integral part of release; this time the sounds are proportionally large and loud in volume. Yells and shouts from the throat to begin with, but as the release deepens, so does the sound, to a roar from deep within the belly.

The rhythm of this release is sudden, electrifying and, because of the energy and sound, often very shocking to a witness in its concentrated forcefulness. It is often also a shock to the person concerned to discover that they had such enormous noise and force within them. The release is intense, powerful and, most importantly, *short-lived*. It is like an eruption. A huge force that subsides quickly, authentic anger has its beginning and its end; unlike unexpressed and therefore unreleased anger, it doesn't rumble on indefinitely. The person releasing anger will sense completion if permitted to express it naturally. The flames reach a peak and then die down. The tension will go if the release parallels the arousal. It may take a little while for the energy to subside completely, but eventually the body and psyche will return to normal.

Safety ⟵—————————————————⟶ Risk

The texture and release of fear. The bodily cues which signal the arousal of feelings of fear, excitement and anxiety again progress from low arousal to high arousal depending on whether we are feeling a mild anxiety or sheer terror. The words we use to describe the feelings associated with this polarity convey their psychosomatic substance: nervous, tense, jumpy, shocked, blood running cold, butterflies in the stomach, a cold sweat. The muscles around the neck and shoulders tighten and the hands may go rigid with knuckles tensing against the fear.

Just as the release of grief occurs with relaxation, so the release of fear occurs when the body stops fighting against the emotion. Here the release is accompanied by trembling, ranging from mild to vigorous depending on the depth of the release: a shivering along the skeleton, and especially up and down the spine, towards the extremities; the muscles of the jaw may tremble, making the teeth chatter; the skin may pale and feel cold, often with a light sweat.

If permission is given and taken for the release to progress, it will escalate and again sounds will be a natural accompaniment. These may start as soft moans, and become shouts, and as the breathing deepens there may be screams if the fear progresses to terror.

The natural rhythm of fear is quite different from that of grief or anger. Instead of the smooth undulation of grief and the explosive force of anger, the pace and rhythm of fear is uneven, jagged, quicker, with varying and unpredictable intensity in the spasms of release. But, as with the other emotions, the release of fear has its own momentum, a beginning, a climax, a descending and an ending point. After the main release is over, there are often sudden but short-lived spasms or shivers or tingles down the spine as the residual tension is dispersed. This may continue over a period of

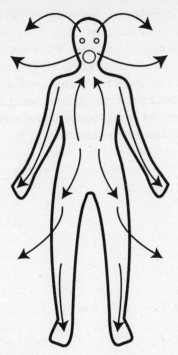

Figure 6   *Emotional release*

minutes or hours and you may feel cold for a while but eventually your body returns to normal.

When the process of emotional release is complete, there is a restoration of well-being and relaxation, a decrease in tension and a renewed energy for life. This point of resolution or restoration occurs in both mind and body. We get glimpses of this when we feel better for having had a good cry or for getting something off our chest or for having a good scream.

If we are able to release fully the accumulated psychosomatic tension – muscular and chemical build-up – the release will be felt as complete. The resolution will be an experience of balance: as the psychosomatic tension subsides, the mind clears of distortions, the perceptions are sharpened, and the whole system returns to normal.

By now, it may strike you that what I am describing as the natural process of emotional release actually sounds alien and strange. The idea of sobbing or shouting or shaking to release emotion may feel as remote a possibility to you personally as growing wings.

This is because, as adults, we have lost touch with this natural mechanism.

The process of emergence, arousal and release just described is interrupted so often and so forcefully by the experience of growing up that not only do we learn not to release emotions, but we lose touch with the physicality of emotion – losing awareness of the body-mind link. First the bodily connection recedes so that we talk about feelings as if they were mental events, occurring only above the neck, and then even mental awareness recedes so that we lose awareness of ever experiencing feelings – they simply disappear from conscious life altogether.

7 | Inhibition and obstruction

To glimpse the unaffected and straightforward progress of the natural cycle of emergence, arousal and release of emotion, we have to look back to the spontaneous behaviour of very young children. The younger the child, the closer she/he is to the natural progression of emotion because the psychosomatic mechanism is intact and has not yet been split into mind over matter.

Most of us lose the childlike qualities of immediacy and unselfconsciousness in our emotional responses by the time we are adults. One reason for this is that we don't feel safe enough: we anticipate such behaviour as embarrassing or even offensive to others. For all of us, whether adults or children, **safety** is a prerequisite for emotional release. We cannot release emotion without it because safety and release go hand in hand.

Safety means absence of threat: threat of death, hurt, danger, punishment, rejection or mockery. The psychosomatic organism needs to feel safe. If either the body or the mind is under threat, release of emotion will not occur. There are many situations in life where safety is absent, for all sorts of reasons.

In a crisis. In an emergency situation, the need to release is suspended. The need to survive takes priority and we enter into a state of complete alertness to the task at hand. We focus all our mental and physical energy on finding help, getting away from, or removing, the danger.

A man drives himself to the local hospital, knowing that something is seriously wrong with him and keeps functioning long enough to park the car, to tell the receptionist he hasn't the time to fill in forms, to insist on urgent help, to get to the emergency team and *then* he collapses.

A woman loses her child in a busy shop and the waves of panic will be suspended while she searches, finds out how to give an announcement, her eyes looking everywhere, all the time barely breathing until her child reappears, at which point she then lets go and releases some of her terror in a mixture of tears and reprimands.

After a close bereavement, we can deal with the essential practicalities and function as long as necessary. Only *afterwards* do we allow ourselves to collapse with grief.

Chronic stress situations. Living in a violent domestic relationship or amid the effects of terrorism and hostility, living in a stage of siege or famine or devastation or incarceration necessitate the use of all our bodily and emotional resources simply to survive. There will be no possibility of release until after the threat or danger has passed.

Ongoing maintenance. It is not only in crisis situations that emotional release is suspended. While the psychosomatic organism is under stress, the mechanism of release is suspended because we need every bit of physical and mental energy simply for ongoing maintenance, in response to the stresses of ordinary life. These comprise the unrelenting demands of getting up, going to work, negotiating traffic jams, producing meals, shopping, attending meetings, pleasing the boss, watching your back, eyeing the competition, making enough money, fighting illness, making ends meet, getting the children through school, worrying about the future. As long as we are using all our energy on maintenance, release of emotion will remain suspended.

Fulfilling obligations. Professional responsibilities take an added toll. A doctor who has to manage the emergency needs of patients; a soldier who has to remain upright and function rationally amid the horrors of war; a counsellor who has to remain detached and objective while processing the tragedies and heartbreak of people – all keep going without release of emotion because they *have* to as part of their duties.

Conscious control of emotion is necessary much of the time. Whatever our level of awareness, we can hold back from release by *intentionally* choosing to restrain the momentum and suppress the release. For personal, professional and socially appropriate reasons, we have to control our emotional release at times. We intentionally hold back from releasing a build-up of irritation towards a child; we intentionally hold back tears in the middle of an office meeting; we intentionally discipline the effects of fear when we need our rational and professional skills to be functioning.

Unfortunately, though, problems occur when this control

becomes permanent. When the emergency is over, when there is a break from the need to be responsible, even when we could release, most of us don't. Not fully. This is because, at the same time, at a much less conscious level, there is another process in operation which causes us to *unintentionally* hold back expression and release of feeling, not through choice but through shame, embarrassment and a deep fear of the punitive consequences. Because of the cultural conditioning described in Chapter 1 and all that we have absorbed about the childish and painful and dangerous aspects of emotion, we suppress our release because of a deep anxiety about losing control. This is why the complete cycle of emergence, arousal, release and *restoration* has become unfamiliar.

If anything does emerge, it is unlikely that release will be complete because we don't feel safe enough. So instead of a feeling of well-being and a sense of psychosomatic restoration, we will often be aware of an uncomfortable residue of mental and physical arousal and agitation, experienced as restlessness, a headache, being stuck, or insufficient physical or mental energy to function properly.

Between the *choice* to control emotional arousal and release in the short-term, on the one hand, because it is not appropriate, and on the other hand, feeling compelled by *fear* to hide, swallow back and suppress the release of emotion for a lifetime, lies a world of difference. For the vast majority of adults, long-term suppression has become the norm.

Part of the reason for this is habit based in attitudes to feelings learned first in childhood. The quality and impact of our learning about emotions in our early and informative years will be the same as our learning about other significant aspects of life: sexuality, death, morality and relationships. It will be deeply ingrained and will influence our behaviour for the rest of our lives.

Whatever our individual experience, most of us absorb directly or indirectly some of the following fundamental precepts about emotion. Whether we are aware of them or not, they are precepts which, learned in childhood, give lasting shape to adult attitudes.

1. Feelings are good or bad.
2. Feelings are caused by other people, usually intentionally.
3. Bad feelings are unwanted and best lied about.
4. Bad feelings are best controlled by denial or a stiff upper lip.

5. Showing feeling is weak.
6. Feelings expressed by adults are devastating.
7. Some feelings are for girls and some are for boys.
8. Some feelings are OK when someone dies or someone cuts in front of you in the car.
9. It's acceptable to blame someone else for your feelings.
10. You can prevent people feeling certain bad feelings if you avoid certain kinds of behaviour and conversely you can induce good feelings by deliberately behaving in other ways.

Through parental, educational, social and cultural reinforcement of these ten precepts, the majority of adults lose touch with the immediacy and the integrity of the natural process of emotional release. Although discipline and discernment are necessary, many of us learn that grown-up behaviour means hiding our feelings and not mentioning them. As we attend to the various roles and responsibilities of adulthood, these beliefs underpin a general tendency to relegate emotional considerations to the bottom of life's pile.

This would not matter as much as it does if we could simply stop having feelings – just turn off a switch and say 'enough now' and stop feeling anything. Medication is one way of achieving this. It is also true that some individuals become so cut off from their feelings that they might be described as being impervious to the effects of emotion. But most of us remain responsive to and affected by life. We cannot escape the emergence of feelings because they are part of being human.

Feelings are aroused even by events that do not impinge on us directly. We are moved by stories of courage and triumph over adversity, touched by myriad forms of love, shocked by images of suffering and despair, frightened by stories of horror and violence, angered by corruption and injustice and our own inability to speak out or change anything. In response to the lament of life and the celebration of life, we *feel* emotions.

We are also subject to emotion through the experience of our relationships. We have feelings in response to the people with whom we live and work, whether we love or hate them, admire or mistrust them. We have feelings in response to the ordinary ups and downs of life, and though we may have neither the time nor the inclination to attend to or even register our feelings, they still affect us.

For many people there are events that are out of the ordinary, traumatic circumstances that can be the first or only time when they recognise they actually *have* emotions. Personal experiences such as watching a friend, child or partner dying of a terminal illness and not being able to help; being assaulted or robbed, sudden injury or involvement in a fatal accident – all cause a lot of emotional disruption.

Remember that emotion is energy moving through the body and psyche with a *purpose*: to restore the psychosomatic balance that is destabilised by high levels of emotional arousal. At the lower end of the cycle of emotional arousal, the disturbance will be slight. We all manage to get through our lives with different feelings arising and declining, emerging and disappearing, bruising or soothing along the way. A stab of envy, a twinge of a old sadness, a familiar irritation with someone, a moment of anxiety, a surge of pleasure and delight, or a recurring sorrow at the loss of someone important from our life: these feelings occur but remain peripheral. They are manageable and we can allow them to ebb and flow without a problem. The arousal isn't enough to interfere with our ability to listen, to work, to behave as we choose; it doesn't affect the way we function.

As we pick up and carry around the small pebbles and the larger stones, the rocks, the boulders, the gems and debris of life's experience, the tension rises. Towards the higher reaches of the cycle, we occasionally hear rumbles threatening an avalanche ahead: the higher levels of arousal will begin to make themselves felt.

What happens when emotional arousal needs an outlet and we insist on keeping the lid on it? How does the body/mind organism cope with the pressure? We may register feeling stressed or over-wrought. This awareness prompts us to make a conscious choice or decision as to how to prevent the level from increasing. At this point, which differs from person to person, we become aware of a build-up of psychosomatic tension caused by the disturbance of this energy.

Physical release. Sometimes our bodies give us clues that the arousal is high. All sorts of aches and pains, many severe, in our neck, head, shoulders, back and legs can be caused by accumulated psychosomatic tension. Often there are far more serious digestive, respiratory or muscular symptoms that alert us. Many people employ and enjoy vigorous exercise to release tension. Even without consciously connecting this need with emotional tension, all

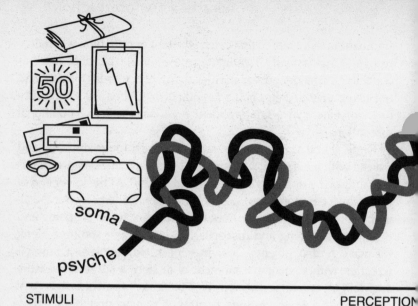

Figure 7   *Blocked emotional arousal*

sorts of energetic activities (sport, dancing, running) and relaxing activities (rest, gardening, fishing) can effectively disperse tension for a while.

Mental release. At other times, we are less aware of anything in our bodies and more aware of being mentally overloaded. This usually prompts a move towards clearing the mind of stressful stimulation. Any activity that helps us personally to switch off is useful in this way. Formal practices of yoga or meditation help to transcend the mental whirrings. Devotees describe a release of memories, thoughts, concerns, associations, a dropping away of the mind, a shifting of consciousness that can allow a state of blissful release.

Diversion. Another important way in which we release tension is by seeking a different and fresh stimulus as a distraction. It may be a temporary change of scene or change of company, going to a film or play or concert, having fun or any way in which we can divert attention away from our preoccupations. This can stimulate a shift of consciousness and a consequent reduction of psychosomatic tension. Sometimes the chosen activity allows for some emotional release as well: a good 'weepy' or horror movie permit us to cry or scream with fear. Laughter, a socially acceptable form of psychoso-

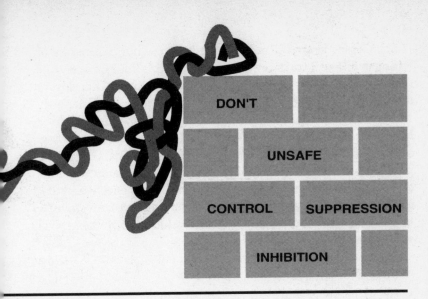

matic release, is especially effective. Allowing ourselves to go with the rhythm of laughter naturally involves the muscles of the diaphragm, and can progress deep into the belly. Sometimes it can have us rocking, doubled up, helpless, even experiencing pain. The restoration of well-being is quite noticeable after 'a really good laugh'.

Laughter is an experience that subverts some of the mental inhibitions we impose on our bodies. Because one of the most noticeable effects of struggling against release is the tightening of the whole breathing apparatus, the actual physiological movement of the diaphragm in laughter can allow release of all kinds of tension. We can find ourselves suddenly surprised by rage or tears and also identify irritation or sadness on the edge of someone else's laughter.

Singing is another activity which can touch on deeper recesses of emotion. In order to sing, we have to breathe, and in order to breathe we have to open and relax the very parts of our body that we have been holding tight. As some of the tension relaxes, emotions can emerge.

For similar reasons, women can experience an emotional release after orgasm: the process of sexual arousal stirs up all sorts of psychological as well as physiological memories and the very vulnerability of orgasm allows access to emotions which can take us by surprise.

Sometimes, instead of release, we suppress our high levels of feeling in different ways. Suppression is possible through alcohol or food or channelling the energy into extra activity. Choosing to numb what you are feeling is, in my own experience, a perfectly valid way of coping under stress on occasions. Sometimes we don't have the time or safety or inclination to address what we are feeling: sometimes it is not appropriate. It is like taking a painkiller for a physical pain: the symptom will be relieved temporarily while the cause remains unchanged. Suppression works very effectively but it offers relief not release. Suppression remains a short-term strategy: in the long-term, the aroused and blocked emotional energy will simply stay there until we address it directly.

Accumulated and blocked emotional energy makes itself felt in a number of ways:

We find that we over-react or under-react to too many things
We find ourselves apathetic or unable to 'cope'
We find it increasingly hard to concentrate

Figure 8   *Emotion blocked in the body*

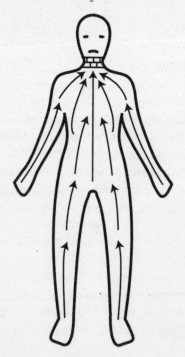

It is harder to keep functioning

Our near and dear ones ask why we've 'changed'

We find ourselves unable to love, to feel close, to give affection, to enjoy sex

We feel disengaged, unreal, disconnected from our life

We find ourselves bursting into tears or losing our temper with little apparent cause

Recognition that the pressure is, in fact, *emotional* helps us to find more direct ways of expression: we may choose to 'have it out' with the person concerned, or talk things through with a close and trusted friend, or arrange to do this with a professional. Putting feelings into words at this stage is a direct and effective way of reducing tension because it actually acknowledges the emotional component.

This will be effective if the emotions concerned come close to matching the stimulus. The toy breaks, the child cries, releases thoroughly, and goes on to something else. A simple, uncluttered process. However, this is a process that belongs to childhood because there has been less time for emotional silt to build up and block the psychosomatic channels. This 'pure' response is virtually impossible in adulthood for most of us because of a process called *restimulation* – a psychosomatic virus that creates havoc in our lives rendering this kind of purity of emotional response impossible.

◆ Read again the ten precepts on pages 65–6, and highlight any that you recognise as having influenced your own attitude to feelings. Use * for what you consider a mild influence, ** for considerable influence, and *** for what you believe is an undying conviction.

◆ What forms of release, if any, do you employ? Do you use these on a regular basis or only when a crisis occurs?

◆ Do you find it easier to release one emotion more than another or are they all equally difficult?

---

8 | Restimulation

RESTIMULATION is an indispensable concept. When we looked at the emergence and arousal of emotion (Chapter 5), we saw how perception increases arousal and arousal in turn influences perception in such a way as to increase the possibility of arousal.

If we return to the analogy of the sexual response cycle, we are aware that we become sexually aroused when we experience a certain image, person, perfume, form or shape, or being touched in a certain way. All of these stimuli can trigger conscious and unconscious memories, associations, images, fantasies that quickly translate physiologically into the process of sexual arousal.

The same process occurs emotionally: a touch, a form, a smell, a voice, an accent, someone's face or manner or walk or behaviour can trigger an emotional response. Often we are quite aware of these associations and as long as we can see clearly that memories are playing a part in our interaction, we can manage perfectly well and adjust our responses accordingly.

Often these associations and feelings from the past intensify feelings in the present. This can cause an escalation of emotional arousal which, without our awareness, will translate into an intensification of anger, sorrow, fear, tenderness or hurt. The very nature of its unconscious and rapid escalation means that we are often un-aware of the process as it is happening but we become aware of the consequences, when we find ourselves in a restimulated emotional state.

One discernible sign when we are responding to restimulated feelings from the past is a clear sense of disproportion and irrationality.

When we are restimulated, we are *over-* or *under-*reacting to a stimulus in the present. Can you identify with any of the following?

> You feel utterly *compelled* or *repelled* by someone you have just met.
>
> Someone overtakes you and, instead of feeling irritated, you want to *murder* the driver.

A friend comments negatively on your new curtains and, instead of feeling mildly disappointed, you feel like *bursting into tears*.

You go to ask your boss for a day off and you don't feel merely anxious but *sick with fear*.

A colleague puts you down in front of others and instead of expressing outrage, you *smile sweetly and murmur agreement*.

Your wife says she doesn't feel like making love and you respond like a *rejected three-year-old*.

Your dinner party is not a success and you feel *suicidal* for days afterwards.

A very close friend dies and you feel absolutely *nothing*.

The inconvenience of narrowly missing your train is magnified into *catastrophic despair*.

Problems occur when these associations and memory triggers are less conscious. When we lose sight of being restimulated and convince ourselves that we are responding only to the present, when reality becomes entangled with assumption and imagination coloured by past experience, the result is a potent and confusing muddle.

For Sharon, the immediate focus and stimulus of her deep distress was the end of a relationship with a man she had met five years before. They had moved in together with their respective children from previous marriages but, for all sorts of reasons, her partner had decided that he wanted out. He left and set up home elsewhere. Sharon felt cheated, angry, humiliated and obsessively determined to avenge herself on him in some way. She had been taking anti-depressants for several months and her children and her friends didn't know how to help.

She felt unable to cope with her life – to look after her children, her home or anything. Life had ceased to be worth living. Talking to her, it soon emerged that twelve years previously, her husband had died suddenly in a car crash, leaving her with two small sons. At the time, she had had to keep herself together just to survive. She had never grieved for her husband whom she loved dearly. A little later she said that her father had died suddenly from a heart attack when she was fourteen. Her mother had fallen apart and Sharon had felt she needed to be strong and look after her mother, so she had never grieved for the father she had adored. Her sole focus was this ex-partner's treatment of her and how she could exact revenge. She was unaware of any connection between her unexpressed and unreleased feelings from the past and her current inability to move from a disproportionate response to her situation.

One of the components of emotional arousal is the influence of past experiences and our conscious or unconscious connections with that past. Once we accept this, we encounter the uncomfortable possibility that what we feel is, in fact, more to do with what we carry around *within* ourselves: an emotional ragbag of memories, associations, unexpressed and unreleased feelings and emotions from past experiences. More often than not, below the threshold of full consciousness, these unresolved emotions move us towards situations and relationships and entanglements with others as a way of offering an opportunity for acknowledgement, expression and resolution.

Even if the term restimulation is new, the existence of connections between past experience and present behaviour is well known. The process of discovering and analysing these very connections is the basic material of all kinds of therapy. Unfortunately, therapy is neither appropriate for nor available to everybody. Because of the impact of the rational/emotional divide in the culture, for many people the very idea of looking at or linking present behaviour with past experiences smacks of indulgence, navel-gazing, being sick, having bad blood in the family. It is seen as time-wasting and utterly irrelevant to life.

However, this inability to see the relevance of connections does not prevent the build-up of emotion. Emotional arousal can accumulate beyond manageable levels: things reach a critical point in our health or work or relationships and we realise something is wrong. It doesn't happen often but it does happen. Because of our habitual dissociation from our bodies, we tend to be caught by surprise when things get to this point, even though tension and psychosomatic stress may have been building for a time, while we ignore the signs.

When someone is completely overwhelmed by a situation and fails to recover or even want to recover from a particular trauma, restimulation is usually the cause. Bill was a policeman, forty years old, happily married for eighteen years and the father of two teenaged children. He was a kind and sensitive man, until something happened at work: he was passed over for promotion and found himself having to take orders from a much younger man. This trigger proved disastrous.

It was nothing directly related to the incident at work. Often a blow of some kind can act as a catalyst. When something interrupts our everyday emotional management, underlying insecurities are stirred up and rise to the surface, manifesting themselves in different ways. For Bill, the experience of being overlooked restimulated some deep emotions, but he didn't know what or why. Slowly but surely, Bill's character seemed to change. He started to drink heavily. His relationships deteriorated: he became extremely spiteful towards his wife and withdrawn from his children.

His wife pushed him to go to their GP. He went reluctantly and was prescribed strong sleeping pills. He was unwilling to speak about anything, except to repeat his bitterness about his unfair treatment at work. Clearly his treatment had been unfair but what was the cause of his response? It was his wife who first talked to me, when she was so desperate and frustrated that she could see no other solution than to separate and break up the family. She had no idea, and neither did Bill, that what accounted for his extreme response was restimulation. It emerged very soon while talking to her that both Bill's parents had been alcoholics. His response to this had been to get away from home as soon as possible. The connections between this fact and his currently disintegrating life were completely obscured in Bill's mind. He hadn't seen his parents for twenty years, so what relevance had his childhood to his life now, his rational self insisted? His emotional self was swamped by all sorts of feelings – past and present, entangled together – and it was only when he joined an AA group that he started to see some of the emotional connections for himself.

When we see these connections, in other words, when connections emerge into conscious awareness, a first and important step is taken. Denying the past because it has no relevance to the present is understandable given our conditioning, but it causes us a great deal of tension and suffering psychosomatically. This is because emotion doesn't occur only at the level of thought, as we have seen. It occurs within the body as well.

The mind–body memory

We need to start again by seeing emotion as a medium – not a concrete object or reality but a fluid state of mental and physical being – that occurs in response to a perception. This state of being has a purpose: to restore pyschosomatic balance to the human organism. Balance is achieved by the passing through of emotion as if through a permeable membrane. The natural response to the arousal of emotion will, if permitted, allow the motion to rise, pass through and over, like a wave. When emotional release occurs, the chemicals aroused into the various organs and systems of the body are also released. The excess, unused chemicals are dispersed and eliminated. With release the perceptions, distorted by arousal, can be clarified. A state of equilibrium is restored.

Once release is hampered or blocked, the process of somatic accumulation begins: the chemicals build up and affect whatever system is vulnerable in the individual. Imagine the effects of stopping release of other waste products from the body and the resulting accumulation of toxins that would soon play havoc with our normal functioning. Emotional chemical accumulation affects us in a similar way, interfering with our bodily and mental systems (see chapters 15 and 16). What we are looking at now is the interference with our heads and our hearts, in others words, the interference with our cognitive and emotional functioning.

When an emotion is not allowed expression, it is 'frozen', suspended as if in a block of ice, felt but not released. Suspended in memory also are the sensations prompted by the event: the sights, sounds, colours, tastes, textures and, as the *medium* in which everything is suspended is frozen, the entire memory is recorded and stored in its pristine, unrefined state, psychosomatically, in our brains and muscles. This applies to single, serial, minor and major experiences.

What is also frozen and recorded is our *perception* and that perception is usually distorted. As I have explained, when we are very young, we are prone to fantastical impressions anyway. Even as older children, we are unable to understand or conceptualise. Instead, we imagine all sorts of things: that we have caused someone harm, even to die; that we are evil inside; that our parents hate us; that being alone means we might die. The perception is distorted until there is an opportunity for release to occur.

Release in the mind and body would allow the whole frozen episode to thaw, to disintegrate and then be sifted through and ordered enough for wrong conclusions to be corrected and more appropriate meanings substituted. Without release, without movement, the perception is emotionally distorted and that is how it is fixed – crude and unprocessed, the imaginary muddled with the real.

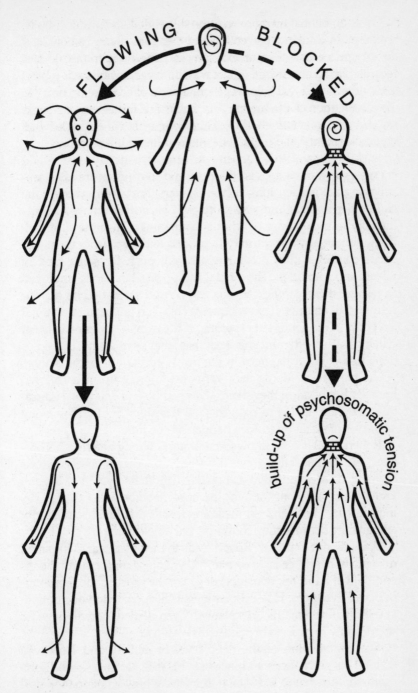

Figure 9   *Emotion as medium*

While emotional memory remains suspended, in our mind–body, it affects our thinking, perception and therefore all our responses. If an experience or series of experiences have been traumatic and recorded, fixed and frozen in this way, our urge towards self-protection and survival will help us generate ways of adapting in order to avoid repetition of the trauma. Our behaviour influences our thinking and this again influences our behaviour; a permanent cycle based on a fundamental and original flawed and immature perception.

A child's instinctual capacity to sense emotional tension and energy as an animal does is still intact and so children are often sensitive to parental tensions, concerns, fears, hostilities. And yet the child's perceptions and sensations will be *further* aroused by the inability to make sense of what is happening. The arousal of feelings, without any opportunity to process and learn from them, can create conflict within a child which will push for some kind of release and resolution. The mental and physical methods employed to resolve these conflicts in our early years set the scene for our future adult emotional management. This is so important because it isn't only in the abnormal experiences, the extreme cases of abuse or cruelty that so often hit the headlines, that permanent damage is done to a child. It happens in the most ordinary of circumstances where parents are doing their very best to bring up their children lovingly but because they themselves had no real emotional education, they are unable to pass this on. Consider the two following examples of situations which happen all the time.

Robert is seven and knows something is wrong between his parents. He hears tense tones of voice, overhears angry words exchanged, sees different expressions in their eyes. He doesn't know what is wrong or why because nobody will explain. His inquiries are met with well-meaning denials that fuel his insecurity and anxiety because they contradict his whole being.

This attempt to protect Robert leads to increased fear in his small dependent heart. He is, of course, too young to comprehend the ins and outs of adult relationships, or grasp the finer nuances of interpersonal dynamics. However, as long as his perception of emotional disturbance remains unexplained, even denied, he will have no opportunity to process or release his own fear.

The combination of the deep level of anxiety and insecurity distorts his perceptions and increases his fear. He imagines all sorts of possibilities based in fantasy. Remember how emotional arousal distorts mental perception which in turn increases the arousal.

Robert's imagination is fuelled by the distorting effects of arousal. The opportunity to talk, to express his feelings safely, perhaps in simple words, and to release them through tears and trembling, would physically allow his body to restabilise and balance, psychologically, his perception would be changed in the light of information and reassurance. Without information, a vacuum is left which is automatically and permanently filled by the naive assumption of *self-blame*. This assumption at least provides Robert with immediate relief from the fear of living with the unknown.

This is one of the common cognitive distortions that occurs in response to such an intense level of fear. The level becomes intolerable and once the 'It's my fault/I'm to blame' connection is made between our brains and the experience of the emotion, it offers a relief from fear. Once the connection is made, it can be made again and again, to reduce fear whenever it is restimulated. This route becomes an alternative pathway that, if reinforced many times over the years, will be evident in the behaviour and attitudes of Robert as an adult. If the connection is made early enough and often enough, this adaptive response of self-blame will seem to the adult Robert, not only a familiar response but perfectly natural. Even if it remains outside his awareness, the adaptive response will influence his behaviour in a multitude of ways as we'll see in the next chapter.

The second example concerns a specific change in circumstance, such as the arrival of a younger sibling.

Laura is four. The arrival of a baby sister and the loss of undivided attention have evoked jealousy, insecurity, anger and a deep need for reassurance. Again, because of vulnerability and an immature perception, all sorts of distortions can arise: the wish to kill or annihilate the 'usurper', the imagined terrifying consequences and fear of being abandoned.

If there is an opportunity for Laura to voice, however simply, some of these feelings and, even better, to release some of her rage in a harmless manner while being contained by the love of her parents, her whole psychosomatic mechanism will be able to release the accumulated tension and to restore a balance. Laura will learn that her anger isn't in itself bad or wicked; she will be helped to put her feelings into a different context through information and reassurance.

What happens otherwise is that, without this opportunity and permission, the process of arousal and distortion continues in the same kind of cycle as described before. The anger, fear and hurt can escalate sometimes to a point when they spill out indiscriminately, maybe in an attempt to injure verbally or physically. If this behaviour is then punished, the conviction of her personal destructiveness will be reinforced. Laura's rage and powerlessness in response to the perceived unfairness – not being seen, being punished – will escalate to a point where it cannot be tolerated, so she will repress it.

The impression that she is essentially bad, etched in her psyche, turns the anger inwards and provides relief from the psychosomatic pressure, enabling her to regain her parents' love and survive in the short-term. Every time Laura's anger becomes intolerable, the conviction that her feelings are too powerful and deadly will shut the emotional door. This conviction will probably form the base for adaptive behaviour and attitudes in Laura's adult life, to the extent that the mere idea of ever feeling angry will seem quite unnatural, without any awareness of why this is so. This is because these emotional 'ice blocks' remain intact somewhere in the psyche even if we believe we have forgotten the past. Working over the years, I have seen many adults astonished to find that, in particular circumstances, they could recall in exact detail the circumstances, surroundings and sensations connected with a specific event, even though consciously they would say they could not remember anything at all.

This applies equally to memories of single events or general experiences of joy and pleasure and security, as it does to memories of sadness, frustration and fear. Although it is usually the so-called negative feelings that have been suppressed or frozen for fear of the consequences, this mechanism will affect our recollection and expression of *all* feelings. As adults, many of us find ourselves inhibited even when we want to express 'positive' feelings of joy, elation, pride, delight and love.

This is a lot of information to take in. Not because it is intellectually demanding but because we cannot absorb this sort of information without it touching – restimulating – memories, associations and all sorts of feelings in us. Whenever I teach this as part of a course, I feel immense sadness at the loss of potential and frustration at the lack of education. But there is also the possibility of change. I was heartened recently to read that a group of octogenarians had participated in some research to see if their ageing muscles could be made stronger with regular exercise. They were given a gentle but regular regime to follow at the gym, and within a few months the results showed a stronger and more flexible muscular response. The researchers were surprised; the octogenarians were simply delighted with themselves and determined to continue.

Emotional muscles can change, too, and become more flexible. How this can happen is the subject of Part Three, but before we look at how we can learn to change, we have to see how the process described above actually impinges on our current lives. How does the theory affect the reality? If all sorts of emotions are restricted and frozen, how do they show? Why don't they simply remain hidden away and forgotten?

Basically, unreleased emotion shows in the ways in which we adapt. The earlier the process of *adaptation* starts, the more often it is reinforced, the more deeply it is ingrained, the more powerfully it will become apparent in the patterns that we can identify, as adults, in our own physical, mental and emotional behaviour.

Come Back

Deep inside,
behind that heavy knee I've got today,
lies another, smaller knee,
a little dirty, and scraped.
And within my fingers, all five of them,
lies a small hand, another one,
still a bit anxious, but warm.
And far inside my skull,
in the innermost part,
other thoughts are tingling,
odd and small ones, almost wrapped up tight, but
they're still
breathing. Full of expectation, almost of joy.
Sometimes they itch –
they want to come out and play
hide-and-seek with me. Often – often.
But then they are suddenly gone. I can't
find them again. So many years have passed,
so many heavy layers of time
have settled over everything.
– But come back anyway, all of you. Come back,
and we'll run and hide,
every one, every one.

Rolf Jacobsen, 'Come Back' from *The Silence Afterwards* (Princeton University Press, 1985), translated by Roger Greenwald.

◆ You might like to try this simple spoken exercise. One person speaks for five minutes while the other listens silently. In your five minutes, take a room or place from childhood and describe it in detail. When you start this exercise, practise letting the room come into your mind as if by invitation, rather than deciding beforehand, with your rational mind, which room you think it would be a good idea to explore.

◆ Imagine yourself actually in this place while you describe what you see, smell, hear, touch and even taste. This exercise is intensified if you describe what you are aware of in the present tense.

◆ This is a simple exercise but, if you allow yourself to concentrate on the sensations you are describing, detecting feelings and emotions associated with the place, it clearly illustrates how the mechanism of frozen perceptions actually operates; if you take one thread and follow it, it will lead to one memory and then another memory. Do not do this for longer than five minutes but make a note of any feelings you are aware of.

9 | The formation of survival patterns

W^E establish patterns in every part of our lives: the ways we think, eat, work, make love and organise our lives tend to fall into recognisable sequences or patterns. Some patterns define us as individuals – the familiar shape by which others recognise the total sum of our parts.

Patterns tend to become habitual and we usually become aware of a particular pattern only when we recognise that it has become harmful to us in some way. This can motivate a decision to change an unhealthy eating pattern, for example, or an unproductive working pattern, and to *adapt* accordingly.

Adaptation, in itself, is part of development. We adapt to change: someone who loses her sight, hears more keenly; we learn to be streetwise when necessary; we take things a little slower when older; when we are in a foreign country we adapt to a different lifestyle; a fallen tree blocks the usual path so we go round it. Healthy adaptation is characterised by *flexibility* and *choice* and a wish to enhance our lives rather than restrict them.

This chapter is concerned with emotional patterns – the characteristic shapes of our relationships to ourselves, to immediate others and to the world at large – and how to identify those patterns which, instead of being healthy and life-enhancing, are rigid and unhelpful. These are often futile, usually a waste of energy and mostly beyond our control. They are recognisable as repetitive cycles of attitudes and behaviour that interfere with how we would like to behave. See if you can recognise any of the following:

Getting involved in fruitless projects
Busily and frantically avoiding silence and solitude
Avoiding responsibility for your actions
Choosing to love people who will never return it
Obsession with appearance
Inability to make decisions
A knee-jerk response of aggression

Pulling the carpet from under your own feet
Constantly eating to fill an emotional need
Constant self-negation
Inability to finish anything
Inability to take risks
Being over-critical of others
Inability to let go sexually
Over-dependency on others' approval
Inability to say 'No'
Inability to take pleasure in anything
Inability to stop smiling sweetly at everyone

Habitual patterns such as these are established in all three dimensions of emotional response: in our bodies, our psyches and our behaviour. Interaction with others initially establishes the formation. We have already seen how emotion is frozen because it is unreleased and that what is stored in ice in the memory are all the sense impressions kept intact; that along with the impressions are the perceptions of the experience.

What is also stored, as an integral part of the memory, is the blocked *need*. The need that triggered the emotions becomes fixed and misrepresented because, without the release of the emotion and the opportunity to readjust a faulty perception, we remain psychosomatically out of balance. Emotional adjustments or patterns are an effort to restore that equilibrium, but problems arise because our very efforts to restore balance involve many contortions which, in time, become more and more exaggerated.

The process of adaptation can be long and slow and the effect can be *chronic*. Imagine that, to begin with, there is a hardly noticeable discomfort, a nagging but intermittent pain like that caused by a small seed-corn in the sole of the foot. You don't notice it all the time but it is there so you start unconsciously to move your foot differently to avoid pressing on that particular spot. At first it is easy to adjust your step but although the adjustment feels small, each small adjustment affects another muscle, often without your awareness. Over time, the discomfort registers and so you increase the adjustment.

As the situation develops and the pain increases, the tension and angle of pressure affect the muscles of the other foot, the calf, thigh, hip, back, shoulders, neck until the whole body is involved in compensating for the imbalance established to avoid the primary pain in the foot. A new pattern of walking is established and reinforced over time until the sequence of continuing imbalance reaches a point when the accumulated pain of adjustment persuades us to seek professional help. By that time, the site of the original pain can be a long way from the area of the presenting problem and has probably been consciously forgotten.

Some adaptations are more *acute*. Standing accidentally on a piece of broken glass will be more of a shock to the system because of its suddenness; the wound will require immediate measures to avoid any pressure on the injured foot. Starting to walk again will necessitate extreme caution to avoid making the injury worse and to allow it to heal. For a while, the foot will remain a vulnerable area in need of care and protection. If a different pattern of walking or moving is established and maintained over a period of time, the adaptive muscular patterns may last long after the original wound has healed.

An adaptation may develop in response to a major trauma. Leaving hospital after major surgery, we are aware of excessive and acute vulnerability and the need to recover. All kinds of dietary and mobility patterns will be adapted in the short-term to effect this but the surgery and new physical status may require *permanent* adaptations in lifestyle.

The wheel

To illustrate the formation of emotional patterns, it is helpful to use the image of a wheel. The hub is the frozen emotion; the spokes are the various mental attitudes, thoughts and images that emerge from the hub and also feed back into it; the outer wheelband is the pattern of our behaviour that keeps the whole adaptive cycle in motion.

The hub: emotional core

At the centre of the wheel is the hub from which radiate the spokes and around which they pivot. In this context the hub represents blocked, unreleased emotion and unresolved need. This emotional energy remains as an unprocessed substance because it has not been dissipated by release and resolution. Containing the suspended

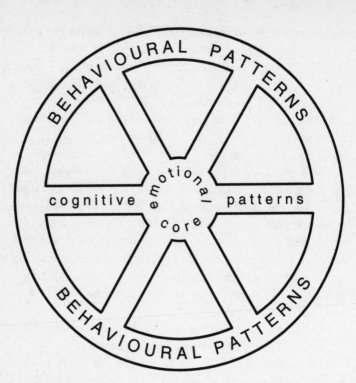

Figure 10   *The wheel*

memories and perceptions, the hub generates the psychic momen-tum that both shapes the individual's adaptive attempts to achieve release and maintains the motion.

The spokes: cognitive patterns

From the hub of the wheel emerge spokes which connect the original needs and emotions with our actual behaviour. These spokes take the form of mental messages, images, thoughts, voices and beliefs about ourselves. Many of these spokes actually reinforce and shape our responses and expectations that make us behave in certain ways; the outcome of this behaviour will in turn reinforce the mental messages. Examples of these cognitive patterns will be included here in each of the polarities but we will look more closely at their disruptive power and effect in Chapter 18.

The wheel band: behavioural patterns

These describe our attempts to restore psychic balance, the energy from the hub mobilising, influencing, colouring and shaping our individual adaptations. The variety and complexity of our behaviour patterns are infinite, but there are some common recurring themes.

1. *Exaggeration.* This theme describes the way in which the child within pushes towards the frozen unmet need but in ways which, as an adult, are extreme, distorted, exaggerated and often inappropriate.

2. *Concealment.* Again, the child within moves to meet the unfulfilled and frozen need from the past, but more covertly, to avoid vulnerability, using some form of cover for self-protection.

3. *Avoidance.* When the experience of unresolved distress is intolerable, we sometimes find ways of avoiding situations or encounters in which these feelings would be restimulated to any degree.

4. *Denial.* Patterns of denial also enable us to avoid stirring up the unresolved need and accompanying emotions but, instead of a complete shutdown, we tend to compensate by moving in the opposite direction.

In the following section, the three polarities are viewed in turn even though, in the same way that our emotions interweave, our patterns interweave. These themes occur singly and in combination, but the patterns which emerge in response to particular emotions and their respective unmet needs have been separated out for ease of recognition.

Closeness ⟵———————————⟶ Separateness

Emotional core. At the centre here is the blocked and unreleased emotion of **grief**, which can take on a life of its own, generating a constant sense of sadness, unnamed loss and emptiness. Disconnected from its source, the free-floating energy becomes distorted into a generalised lack of self-love, a belief that we are somehow rotten or unlovable at the core, that we don't deserve happiness. We experience a chronic pessimism, a tendency to disappointment, a sense that the grass is always greener elsewhere:

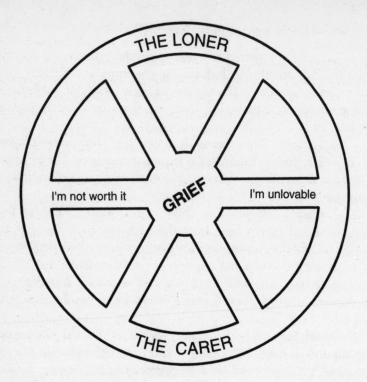

Figure 11   *The wheel with grief at the hub*

and because the sadness is unreleased, it often assumes the form of an abiding loneliness.

Cognitive Patterns

Some recognisable 'messages' that affect the way we behave are:

'I'm unlovable.'
'They couldn't manage without me.'
'Poor me.'
'I'm ugly/a mess.'
'You've got to look happy.'
'I'm not worth it.'

Behavioural patterns

Exaggeration. We try to resolve our need for love and closeness as adults, but the 'child within the adult' behaves in ways which are inappropriately needy, excessively demanding and possessive. We want so much to be loved and to give love that we find ourselves clinging on to situations and relationships that have lost their life and nourishment because we fear so much the pain of aloneness.

The unrequited need for *self*-love and separateness becomes distorted into patterns of self-obsession, self-pity and a preoccupation with how we are *seen* in particular and our psychological or physical state in general. We are prone to an inflated sense of importance, as if the self, like a balloon constantly deflated in childhood is so limp and ill-defined that it has to be pumped up with hot air, simply to keep it from collapsing again. A curious vanity can emerge: using our internal mirrors exclusively as a protection against the uncertain reflection from external mirrors, our self-image becomes a distortion which, in turn, distorts the reflection of those with whom we interact.

Concealment. When grief charges our unmet needs for closeness, we try to meet these needs without opening ourselves up to the risk of more hurt. Entering into a marital partnership, perhaps, but choosing someone whose culture and language is alien enough to prevent truly intimate contact; going through the motions of a relationship but without being accessible or open emotionally, being there but not there; playing the field sexually in order to meet the need for contact but never staying around long enough to risk getting too close *or* too separate. As honesty is an integral part of closeness, *dis*honesty becomes inevitable: for example, compulsive extra-marital encounters or never being able to make love to your partner without using sexual fantasies about another person.

The energy from unresolved needs for separateness give rise to patterns of dependence in the guise of independence. Though professing a 'take it or leave it' attitude, we depend on a partner to be the emotional cipher, the go-between, the one who 'has all the feelings' so that we can remain safely on the outside.

Avoidance. Stuck in the belief that closeness with other human beings is dangerous, the child within shuts down on any contact that risks stirring up old hurt. We avoid the need to love: the need to share love with others and the need for self-love. Characteristic **loner** patterns of behaviour emerge: emotional withdrawal, alienation, distancing and restraint from affectionate touch with partner or friends or children; choosing work which will necessitate long periods away from home so that a 'justifiable' distance can be maintained.

We may develop our lives around an overt preference for isolation rather than close contact with others. Some of us find a comfortable niche in working with facts and inanimate objects; we choose work that involves us in the intimacy of another human being's body or psyche but within safe clinical constraints. We may find it easier to express affection to animals than humans; we may collect inanimate objects or become excessively drawn to computers, preferring closeness with others through a screen over real-life encounters.

Denial. The energy from past unreleased grief is powerful. One of the ways it affects us is to make us deny our need to be loved. This gives rise to **carer** patterns which are characterised by an appearance of self-sufficiency, while giving endlessly to others. This behaviour creates an increasing imbalance as the denial arouses our hidden sadness and desperation even more. The care, at root, is real and authentic, but the original grief and hurt push more and more for release with such a frightening force that we feel unable to voice our own needs, through fear of overwhelming others and eliciting more rejection and hurt.

Other patterns of over-dependence emerge when we deny the possibility of separateness and *self*-love. Separateness looks as inviting as a black hole of non-existence. Identity and meaning of self become so bound up with the others in our lives that we avoid being true to ourselves so as not to risk rejection. Grief disfigures our perceptions so that we become convinced we are basically a *reject*, to the extent that we anticipate and even provoke rejection from others.

Our inability to be separate makes it difficult to allow others to be alone. We intrude because we cannot appreciate the necessity for solitude; our own need to be indispensable can make it hard for us to accept that others have separate identities with separate feelings, moods, thoughts and wishes which have nothing to do with us. Similarly, we find it difficult to love others as they *are*, to respond to the reality of someone else's needs instead of what we imagine them to be.

Overall distortion. One way to detect a major pattern in operation is when the unmet and frozen need feels more like a threat than fulfilment. Separateness will no longer be equated with self-loving and time spent by choice on our own: it becomes the unwelcome spectre of loneliness and rejection. A place of self-nourishment and love becomes distorted into abandonment and hurt. Similarly, when the unmet need is for closeness, it will be distorted into a smothering, overwhelming, dangerous prospect instead of an opportunity to share the joys of loving.

Engagement ←——————————→ Containment

Emotional core. Here at the hub is the unreleased and frozen emotion of **anger**. When the release of natural anger is prevented or punished, the push to assert the self is not met and matched by the other: it is blocked. In other words, this push is met with oppression and experience of powerlessness. As long as the anger remains blocked, the powerlessness persists. Sown in that sense of utter powerlessness as a consequence of someone's greater power over us is the seed of our own aggression.

What happens inside completes the establishment of a lifelong pattern. The energy of anger is quite different from that of grief or fear: it is volatile, fiery, sudden and often shocking. It feels large. The combined effect of the energy of this particular emotion with no release causes an overwhelming pressure that becomes intolerable, threatening our own survival. The only way out is to escape from the powerless position by transforming the energy into hatred and blame. This is directed outwards: the blocked energy fosters fantasies of omnipotence and destruction as we identify with those in a position of power over others, until we fear being so destructive that we imagine destroying the very person we depend on, or being destroyed ourselves in retaliation. Fear of the consequences of our rage makes us redirect it towards a new and safer target: ourselves. It then is compounded by blame for being so weak.

Another way to relieve the intolerable pressure is to shut down. Sometimes a child will withdraw completely from all engagement as a means of psychic survival. More often we continue to engage but with no experience of equality. We absorb the rules of aggression and alleviate our unexpressed anger about the injustice we experience ourselves. We find ways to exert that same sort of power over others, starting with smaller beings like animals or younger children or toys, shaping the patterns of aggressive behaviour for the future.

With continued lack of release, the energy of anger – the need to assert and develop the self within the boundaries of others –

accumulates at the emotional core. But by adulthood it has become so inextricably interwoven with and distorted by aggression that it is difficult to separate them out in experience.

Two factors allow us to mistake aggression for anger. The first is the cultural pattern of competition. The sanction of aggression as a natural, healthy and normal aspect of human development conditions us to anticipate every single interaction in our lives as a potential contest from which one has to emerge as winner and the other as loser. This has spread from competitive games, where rules require a winner and loser as an integral part of the format of the particular sport, to relationships with friends, children, neighbours, strangers, colleagues, clients. Everybody we encounter – in a shop or on a train, on the road, in the workplace or in the privacy of our home – has the potential to be either winner or loser depending on our own skills and strategies. Aggression has become the *norm*.

Second, our experience of other people's 'anger' has usually been

Figure 12   *The wheel with anger at the hub*

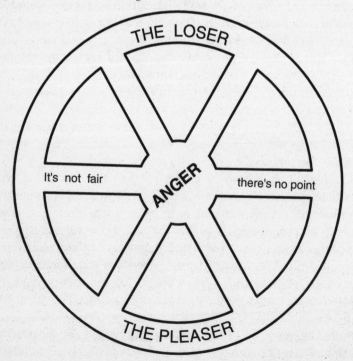

the experience of people's aggression. This may have emerged in physical or verbal violence and abuse or it may have been through indirect but equally hurtful criticism and put-downs: either way, our experience tells us that 'anger' is harmful. Furthermore, despite our best efforts to suppress our own anger because we have confused it with aggression, and fear for its destructive consequences, our own anger *will* emerge because we are human (thank goodness) but it will probably be expressed as aggression. If it is turned outwards, directly or indirectly, we will in fact injure others and will relearn that aggression is destructive. This reinforces our determination to suppress *any* feelings that touch on these areas so that the true pure human and necessary emotion of anger is thrown out with the dirty bathwater of aggression.

Disconnected from the source, the emotional energy at the hub largely appears in the form of a generalised and learned aggression. This alternates between a chronic sense of powerlessness and blame. Blame helps to salve the experience of futility and power-lessness. Whether directed towards others or against ourselves, blame consumes a lot of emotional energy because it can go nowhere: it simply revolves, feeding itself, and as long as this is happening, we cannot put energy into changing the situation.

Cognitive patterns

Some familiar thought patterns based in anger are:

'It's not fair.'
'Don't let them see you're vulnerable.'
'Revenge is sweet.'
'There's no point.'
'I'm to blame.'

Behavioural patterns

Exaggeration. As adults, we move to engage but with the exaggerated and compulsive quality of the child. Consequently, the need to engage changes to the compulsion to *win*. Patterns are characterised by a generally aggressive stance in life: always ready to attack, needing to prove ourselves to all comers whether or not they want to compete. We need to be the boss, the one on top, the bully, because we don't want to experience again the feelings associated with being the underdog, the one at the bottom, the victim.

As lack of containment also elicits anger, even a young child seeks release in provocative and delinquent behaviour, deliberately pushing for the boundaries to be fixed. The child within the adult frame pushes in a similar way. Confusion about our own boundaries charged with past emotion produces patterns of provocation, eliciting others' anger. We invade others' boundaries by intruding or coming too close. Putting our feet on someone's chair, helping ourself to food from someone else's plate, touching someone else's body in an inappropriate manner, leaving our belongings scattered in someone else's 'territory', asking intrusive questions, ferreting around in other people's business are examples. We push and push and talk and talk and don't know when to stop. This may provoke the other person to fury but as this is rarely communicated effectively, these patterns continue. In some instances they develop into the transgression of social boundaries that can result in sanctions and penal 'containment'.

Concealment. We move to engage but we use *covert* weapons so as not to risk direct experience of someone's anger or aggression – or our own powerlessness. The inter-personal arsenal includes sarcasm, malicious gossip and sabotage of anyone else's power with put-downs or excessive criticism.

Collusive behaviour also allows engagement behind a screen. Although the profile we keep may be low, and personal anger may be denied completely, we exert covert power through collusion: we avoid the drama of direct conflict by hiding behind others' aggression either in a group or a partnership. We stay out of the actual arena but our participation, in the audience or behind the scenes, is an integral and essential ingredient of the power play, so that our own aggression achieves an indirect release.

Avoidance. We avoid any kind of conflict by adopting a resigned and compliant stance in life, opting for a blind eye rather than a black eye. We obey orders deferentially, carry out instructions regardless of our own personal beliefs. We stop challenging, daring, risking the arousal of anger in ourselves or others. On constant alert to the possibility of conflict, we avoid arguments and rows. We learn to placate, pour oil on troubled waters, smooth out the wrinkles of life and go along with anything for the sake of a peaceful life and keeping out of trouble.

When the pressure of unreleased anger becomes intolerable, the psychic mechanism loses flexibility and the emotional state of *depression* is often the outcome, and with it an emotional numbness caused by the massive energy turning in on itself. Feeling fundamentally among life's 'losers', we adapt with patterns of self-defeating behaviour.

Feelings of apathy, deadness, hopelessness are usual. The anger closes in to form a prison around our self, a place of *self*-containment, to meet this need without having to engage with or be contained by another person. This prison provides a boundary around our being. Even if misconstrued, it nevertheless offers a respite from battling with what have been distorted into alarmingly destructive forces within our psyche.

Denial. Unclear and inadequate perceptions of the boundaries between self and others lead to over-identifying with others and denying the need to engage or to assert ourselves. We become lost without any markers or outside definition and develop **pleaser** patterns, saying 'Yes' to everything and everyone, taking anything in, psychologically or physically. We find it hard to know the boundary between our own feelings and other people's.

Behaviour becomes indiscriminate: we tend to binge, taking in ideas, opinions, values, food. We give up the facility of choice, giving in to everything, being pushed and shaped by outside forces until the accumulated rage becomes intolerable and the hidden, real, ugly (because angry) self emerges, eliciting feelings of self-loathing. This re-acquaintance with our real self instead of the false self signals a reassuring limit where we know when to stop – for now.

When we deny the need to be contained, we deny vulnerability. Weakness becomes synonymous with powerlessness so we then attack what we identify as weak and powerless in ourselves and others. We do not want to be reminded of early experiences of fear, powerlessness and being out of control.

This leads to abusive patterns of behaviour. These include self-abuse, self-mutilation, anorexia, alcoholism and other addictions. Sometimes this leads to abuse of others on a personal scale: rape, sexual abuse, physical and psychological abuse of women, children and the elderly. With synchronous external and political power, these behaviour patterns extend to abuse of others on a national scale. Dictatorial and tyrannical abuse of the weak and vulnerable can be seen throughout the world. The suppressed energy of anger, transformed into hatred, out of control because unbounded, becomes a vehicle for violence and annihilation of other human 'things'.

Overall distortion. Both aspects of the polarity change so that engagement becomes estranged from its original meaning. Self-assertion, self-expression, the need to be matched and met as an equal become perverted into the anticipation of opposition, of war, do or die, win or lose. Instead of the potential of finding our own boundaries by meeting those of others, containment becomes equated with loss, defeat, annihilation and disgrace.

Safety ⟵⟶ Risk

Emotional core. Absence of fear is trust, in others and in ourselves, which informs us when it is safe to relax and explore and reach out. The purpose of fear is to give us appropriate warning of the risk of psychological or physical harm, of any threat to our well-being.

Figure 13   *The wheel with fear at the hub*

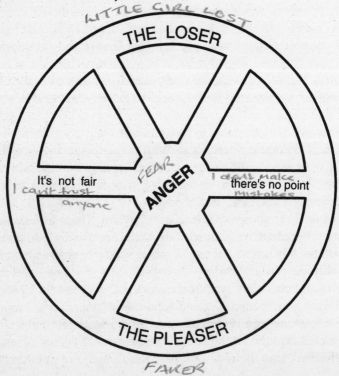

Too little safety and too much unpredictability in the past plus the distorting effects of unreleased fear transform this emotion into chronic *anxiety*. In place of the ability to use its energy to mobilise us into a particular action or performance, this anxiety becomes disconnected from its source, immobilising us in energy-depleting circles.

Unreleased fear has a tendency to take on an inflated life of its own, feeding greedily on our imagination and distorting our perceptions. We lose touch, confusing reality with fantasy, and sometimes becoming paralysed by phobias or paranoia. Fact becomes fiction and fiction becomes fact.

Cognitive patterns

Repetitive beliefs and convictions based in fear which help us rationalise our behaviour patterns include:

'You can't trust anyone.'
'Never make a mistake.'
'Don't show you're afraid.'
'I don't belong anywhere.'
'Don't rock the boat.'

Behavioural patterns

Exaggeration. As adults, we try to establish a sense of safety but, once again, the frightened child within will run the show, so a normal human need becomes distorted and exaggerated by a sense of desperation.

The unreleased fear fuels a chronic anxiety about getting everything right. Not only major but even inconsequential decisions assume the power of life-threatening dilemmas: what to buy for supper? What to wear to the meeting? Will turning right or left be quicker? Which box to tick? We become convinced that we have to find the right words, do the right thing, at exactly the right time or else . . . the actual threat varies but it usually feels dangerous, inarticulable and frightening, overwhelmingly so at times. Habitual patterns assume a placating function: smiling, agreeing, washing, apologising, performing superstitious rituals.

Our natural need for risk can also become exaggerated. Danger can take on an allure of its own: the experience of thrills, the desire for that rush of adrenaline. We may deliberately experiment with danger – working in a high-risk job, competing in a high-risk sport, gambling, taking drugs – seeking any experience which leads us to feel anxiety and fear but in a way which seems within our control. We find ourselves intolerant of routine, fearing being 'pinned down' or stuck in a rut. We are always looking for an escape, a route guaranteed to leave access to freedom.

Concealment. To protect ourselves from harm, we employ a range of psychological guises, costumes and roles. We start off with an insecure sense of self and an imagined sense of other and use different 'appearances', chosen with the particular 'other' in mind. Some familiar examples of these are:

The Little Girl Lost
The Funny Clown
The Seductive Flirt
The Sympathetic Nurse
The Wise Oracle
The Rebel
The Cosy Counsellor
The Black Sheep

We all use roles or masks by choice to some extent, but concealment describes a more extreme pattern: an inability ever to be ourself. It entails a corresponding inability to tune into others' *real* feelings and needs, instead of what we imagine them to be.

Other people risk becoming objects, like so many dolls, arranged on the stage of our own drama, which we move back and forth or remove according to the scripts we've written. It is difficult to know another person from a position of self-trust or to let ourselves be known, because this trust has never been established. The notion of being true to oneself becomes impossible because we become lost in our own roles and our frustration with it periodically turns into despair.

Vicarious living allows us to live through others without risking anything personally. This accounts for the attraction of watching others on the screen risking life and limb, failure or personal exposure, from the comfort of our armchairs. In personal relationships we can do this as well – encouraging children, friends, partners, others to take the risk of changing jobs, sitting an exam, initiating a confrontation with someone, going first, making fools of themselves, having a go. We bask in reflected glory if it works, and are shielded from direct exposure if it fails.

Avoidance. When the level of emotion is intolerable, we tend to avoid risk by cutting it out of our lives completely. We settle for a safe existence, stay with the familiar in the places we know with the people we know, saying only the words that are safe to utter. We prefer to stay hidden within the herd than stray outside.

Whenever fear looms, as it always does despite our precautions, we try to strengthen our sense of confidence by fitting our world into dogmatic and rigid categories of right/wrong, saved/damned, good/bad. The lines between 'them' and 'us' become more rigidly defined. The more fearful we feel, the less we are able to tolerate doubt and uncertainty, and the less we question or are prepared to suspend belief. Prejudice, labels and strict demarcation become the tools of emotional survival. Sometimes we attach ourselves to groups or sects because they appear to offer a safe haven, a place where we can find relief in exclusivity.

Denial. One of the most common patterns of concealing and denying unreleased fear is the use of aggression. Aggression is related to the engagement/containment polarity: the perception of powerlessness, whether real or imagined, can trigger a response of aggression as a smokescreen, or defensive bluff. This can appear in the form of intimidation, in other words, frightening others in order to inflate one's own sense of power. This pattern is based in denial of fear; acknowledging fear and continuing in spite of it constitutes courage.

Unreleased and denied fear can also become a chronic worry that generates patterns of controlling behaviour as we try to avoid the unpredictable. We control ourselves, which can lead to difficulty in letting go emotionally or sexually with a partner, and we need to control others. We can deny our need for risk by trying to keep others emotionally where we need them: not angry or disappointed or beyond our reach. We become unreasonably fearful of changes in others' moods because we haven't been able to build the necessary inner sense of security and balance to survive being shaken by the unexpected and unpredictable in those we love. We manipulate them into decisions or along certain paths that we may believe are for their own good to ensure that everything goes according to 'plan'.

Manipulative patterns are especially hard to acknowledge because of the belief that manipulative behaviour is rooted in some inherent evil in our hearts. Once we understand that these patterns derive from a deep and learned fear and inability to trust, it

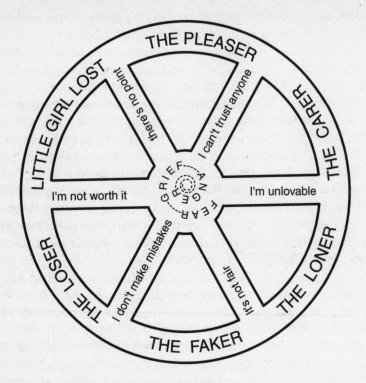

Figure 14   *The wheel: interweaving patterns*

becomes possible to start taking genuine risks and little by little to allow ourselves to experience and release the fear and learn to trust.

Overall distortion. Again, over time and with constant reinforcement, the psychic mechanism becomes rigid and both needs assume a negative and unwelcome aspect: safe becomes stagnant and lifeless, risk appears foolhardy and dangerous. The unreleased anxiety and fear restrict our capacity to learn a natural balance; the more we avoid risk, the less likely we are to feel genuine safety. We lose touch with that vital instinct which informs us of possible danger or safety and we end up putting misplaced trust in others, going against our better judgement and leaving ourselves open to unnecessary harm. Loss of self-trust breeds a chronic worry and generalised mistrust in others and the world at large.

Reading through these examples, you may recognise your own and others' behaviour spanning more than one category and see that these patterns interweave across all three polarities. Usually, we recognise two or three dominant patterns in our behaviour, and other secondary patterns that are shaped as a consequence of continuing adaptation through life. Although some are easily recognisable, others are so deeply ingrained and have become so much part of the fabric of our being that we do not always see them so clearly.

At this point, we can simply leave it at that – an interesting round trip exploring some of the patterns of human behaviour – and conclude that all these interweaving shapes simply reflect the variety of life. Admittedly, patterns of compulsive risk-taking, or withdrawal from people, or the ability to care for others with no regard for ourselves, can work well for us in life and even be socially useful: there are times when we are grateful that someone else is meticulous or generous to a fault.

Yet, there is often a cost of functioning in these ways. These patterns can range from being mildly unhelpful to downright destructive and the blocked emotional energy can cause a great deal of suffering. What is the alternative? Is it possible to manage our emotions differently and to separate past from present? Can we feel more in touch with our emotions and enjoy them more? The next part of this book introduces the possibility of living with these emotional connections without becoming tyrannised or shackled by them.

---

1. Are there any cycles in the list on pages 83–4 that you recognise in your own life? Are there additional ones that apply to you more individually?
2. Look at the section relating to the Closeness–Separateness polarity starting on page 87. Make a note of any behavioural patterns that remind you of your own. Again there is no need to change anything, just to note them and acknowledge the connection with the unreleased emotion.
3. Follow the instructions in 2 above, for the patterns associated with the Engagement–Containment polarity starting on page 91.
4. Follow the instructions in 2 above, for the patterns associated with the Safety–Risk polarity, starting on page 96.

Having understood a little more about patterns, are there any that you feel have a particularly disabling effect on your life?

Part Two

A NEW APPROACH: DANCE

My motivation for writing this book was to put feelings on the map of normal life. I wanted to convey the ordinariness of feelings instead of sensationalising them and to help people see that we regard emotions as obstacles only because we have never learned how to use them as energy.

The first part of this book focused on the effects of past experience on our lives in the present. Part Two looks towards the future. Currently, the decision to explore our heartscape is usually triggered by a crisis or the realisation that we are unable to function as fully as we feel we could. This exploration is usually undertaken with the help of a professional but, while this is often valuable, an understanding of our emotional make-up does not necessarily require professional intervention.

Most of us suffer from a lack of emotional education. As a general consequence of the 'Don't' approach, there are five vital lessons about the management of feelings that few of us have learned:

1. Others do not cause our feelings, so blaming others is a waste of time and energy.
2. Outside triggers act as catalysts only for what is going on in our hearts, helping it to come to the surface so that it can be dealt with safely.
3. Our emotions give us important information about our relationships.
4. We can use the medium of emotion as we do the medium of the intellect; to evaluate, to discriminate, to gain insight into the meaning of our experience.
5. Self-discipline and a measure of self-control are appropriate and possible, while at the same time we should value the expression and release of emotion when necessary.

It is possible to learn to manage and monitor our emotional health and well-being without become obsessive, in the same way that we can learn to manage and monitor our physical health and well-being, making adjustments as we change and develop through life.

We learn to value our physical health and take care of ourselves, keeping active; we learn to value our intellectual health and keep ourselves mentally active. We can enjoy and value and manage our emotions in a similar way.

We focus now on the possibility of exploring and becoming more familiar with our personal heartscape: our areas of sensitivity and numbness, places of pleasure and pain, the influences that help or hinder us in our relationships. I have always believed that people can do so much for themselves if they are given clear information and are encouraged to trust themselves. It is to emphasise the ordinary and natural aspects of emotion that I have shaped the following model. You can use it to monitor, identify, assess, appropriately manage and learn from whatever emotions are present in your life – in order to get on with your life, more fully.

The following sections will describe in detail the model based on the principles of **DANCE** – *a new model of emotional management:*

> **D**istress
> > **A**cknowledgement
> > > **N**aming
> > > > **C**atharsis
> > > > > **E**valuation

Distress – describes the signals that something is out of balance

Acknowledgement – refers to the ability to recognise and accept these signals

Naming – is putting this recognition into words to communicate to someone else

Catharsis – takes us to the next step of releasing emotion when necessary and appropriate

Evaluation – is the ability to choose how to respond to situations with more awareness

These principles stand as alternatives to the current cultural model of emotional illiteracy based on the principles of:

> **D**enial
> > **R**ationalisation
> > > **E**vasion
> > > > **A**ccumulation
> > > > > **D**istortion

Denial – refers to the habit of cutting off from the body's signals with the resulting 'I've no idea what I am feeling' or 'I am not feeling anything'

Rationalisation – describes our physical and mental struggle against emerging emotion

Evasion – is the general reluctance to communicate feelings in a straightforward manner

Accumulation – is the process of the build-up of tension, physically and mentally, occurring when there is no release

Distortion – describes the consequences of accumulation on our behaviour

10 | Distress v. Denial

WHEN a feeling is expressed easily and clearly, whether it be love or happiness or sadness or frustration, we do not experience distress. Distress occurs when we experience strain, a struggle *against* the emerging emotion: whenever there is a felt pressure to prevent expression, this causes discomfort or pain and we suffer a state of imbalance.

Emotional distress signals to us that something is wrong, that the balance needs restoring, and is an indication of *health*, just as our bodies give us other signals which indicate something is amiss and needs attention.

Recognising these physical sensations, recognising that we are feeling *something* even if we don't know what, is the first and vital step in learning to manage emotions. We can learn to recognise and accept these signals of distress as an aspect of healthy functioning instead of denying and suppressing their existence.

Denial is born of dread, a belief that these signals mean danger. Over time, an established pattern of *dis*sociation from our bodies becomes ingrained. We stop listening to what our bodies are telling us because we are afraid of what will happen if we lose control. After years of not listening, we actually lose the ability to hear. We stop noticing what is happening in our bodies so the end result is that we lose touch. When asked what we are feeling, we can reply, 'Nothing' quite truthfully and then discover, long afterwards, that those feelings were there but we simply couldn't register them at the time.

The gap between experience and recognition means that the body and mind have to be reprogrammed into a more effective collaboration. With practice in discerning distress, the gap becomes reduced but it does take time for the links between psyche and soma to become clearer and function more efficiently. Like co-ordinating unused muscles, regular practice is need to strengthen the ability to make the connection.

Denying our feelings doesn't make them go away. As we have seen, the particular emotions causing the distress will operate through our behavioural and mental patterns, but without our awareness and therefore beyond our control.

The first step in emotional management is to notice and observe these signals, like listening to the unfamiliar sounds of an unknown language. It is impossible to begin with any accurate understanding because there are so many layers of suppression in our psyches and most of us, as adults, have become detached from our physical cues.

Start from *within* – notice bodily changes in heat, pressure, tension, and so on, and ask 'What am I feeling?' Then take a moment to wait. The common mistake at this point is to respond to the fear of confusion and muddle by not waiting for an answer from within and instead looking outside for a reference point, trying to gauge from other people what we should be feeling. This only takes us further away from our own reality and will never help us develop the capacity to identify and recognise our interior emotional state.

Step inside your emotional space and look around. Slowly the silence and blank confusion will develop into murmurs and forms that assume a recognisable shape and meaning. Wait until an answer to your question appears, as it will if you are receptive and open.

You are looking for a lead, a clue, like following a thread into a knot. You don't have to get it absolutely right. This isn't a test – it is simply a way of building your awareness and trusting it. It is *for yourself*, this stage.

11 | Acknowledgement v. Rationalisation

WHEN an emotional clue appears, the escape route of rationalisation beckons; we dismiss the clue because the feeling is irrational or stupid, and especially if it is 'negative'. In Chapter 1 we looked at the effect of social conditioning in terms of categorising feelings into 'desirable' and 'undesirable'. This negative/positive division has seriously affected our capacity to recognise emotion. We dismiss or repress what we feel, we rationalise it away as embarrassing or accuse ourselves of being over-sensitive or unworthy of such feelings.

'I shouldn't be feeling this – it's really ungrateful of me.'
'It's silly to be afraid – I'm just pathetic.'
'I've got no right to feel this – I'm probably imagining things.'

This habit of imposing a rational structure on emotional experience interferes with our ability even to recognise emotional clues, let alone process them effectively. The division between 'good' and 'bad' feelings has left us with more anxiety than clarity and the resulting confusion means that our emotional language remains rudimentary. The skill of acknowledgement helps to build a broader and more accurate emotional vocabulary.

This skill describes the ability to identify as accurately as possible what we are feeling. To do this, it is important not to be put off by whatever you find. Learn to trust whatever thread emerges and don't worry *why*. Trust it – the anxiety you first discern may lead to irritation, the hurt you identify could be a cover for resentment. It doesn't matter. Trust your body and psyche and you will find that this skill becomes easier.

An emotional vocabulary: Kites

To help this process of identification, first look more closely at the difference between *emotions* and *feelings*.

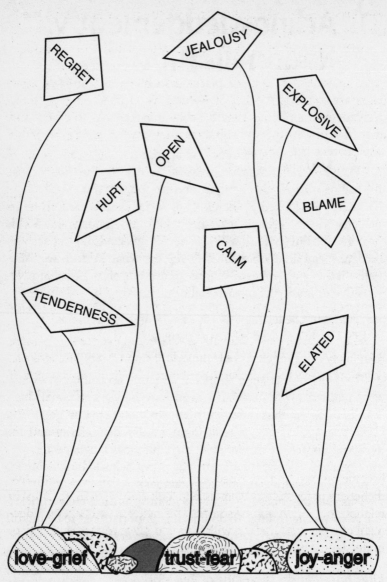

Figure 15   *Kites*

I described grief, anger and fear as the primary emotions, like the three primary colours. Sourced in our animal instinctual needs, they are also experienced by intelligent animals. Because these emotions are part of human existence, they are universal. It matters not when we are born, in what circumstances or what our life experiences are

– we experience these emotions in response to our instinctual needs for love, for power and for trust.

From the bases of these three primary colours arise an infinite range of variations and shades as they blend, intensify, become more concentrated in some places than others. From these three bases arise *feelings*. I think of feelings as social or inter-personal derivatives of emotion. They describe our response to others and arise from our interaction with them; they are part and parcel of our relationship with others in our lives.

Feelings are the currency of our relational lives: examples are guilt, disgust, gratitude, envy, shame, aggression, humiliation, blame, admiration. They are *learned* in the same way that we learn everything else in life: through modelling and social conditioning. Feelings exert a powerful influence on our attitudes and behaviour but they are not necessarily universal. They depend on general culture and particular upbringing and personal disposition. Not everyone feels jealousy, for example; not everyone feels disappointment in the same way; rejection will have different meanings for different people.

When it comes to identifying and naming emotions, it is more than likely that the names of feelings will come first. Feelings act as 'kites', markers flying around in the emotional breeze, which, if their strings are traced back, can be found attached to an emotion at the base. Feelings, in some ways, are more obvious because of our preoccupation with relationships to others, leaving us unable at first to recognise the unheeded deeper emotion.

There are commonly experienced feelings and feeling states that become blurred and confused and although there is no definitive dictionary of feelings, it is possible to look at some of these 'kites' in relation to their emotional source. This helps in our acknowledgement of what is happening within us and gives us the possibility of understanding a feeling in its deeper context.

Kites based in the emotions of love and grief

A *feeling state* emanates from physiological sensations that can be directly translated into a nameable feeling: pleasure–warm–open–cosy–expansive–radiant–tender and cold–withdrawn–closed–hurt–gutted–heartbroken–shattered–heavy–numb are some examples which illustrate the psychosomatic nature of feelings associated with the closeness/separateness polarity.

Regret when authentic, differs from guilt and is deeper than feeling apologetic. Regret and *remorse* belong here because they are concerned with loss: loss of opportunity, an opportunity denied to give, share or receive love and care. Loss of what might have been or what was and is no longer are sources of real *sorrow* for us all at different levels and moments in our lives. We regret those opportunities lost through our actions or our omissions or the neglect of ourselves or others. The grief usually needs acknowledgement and release before we are able to move through this state and onwards.

Apology, when genuine, is attached to regret. However, the compulsive gestures of apology, of which we seem inordinately fond, become more of an automatic response than an expression of sorrow. This response is related to hierarchical positioning. As animals adopt submissive postures when they wish to placate a threatening or superior animal, so humans adopt apologetic stances as a socially learned defence against aggression and displeasure. When apology becomes detached from authentic sorrow, it acts frequently as a significant clue to the emotion of underlying anger, not grief.

Vulnerability literally means the ability to be wounded and is included here because it is often misused. From a hierarchical perspective, vulnerability has become synonymous with powerlessness. Powerlessness has assumed unwelcome, even despised, connotations associated with defeat. Being powerless can leave us with little or no protection against hurt, inspiring in others corresponding feelings of compassion and care. However, the legacy of aggression has distorted the ability to honour vulnerability.

From a non-hierarchical perspective, vulnerability has a power and a value, dependent on *personal* power, the ability to be true to oneself rather than powerless in a competitive context. Reflecting on this feeling more specifically can therefore be helpful: am I really feeling vulnerable and therefore need to protect myself realistically in some way; or am I feeling powerless and afraid to assert my own power?

Compassion is a composite feeling deeply rooted in love and, more importantly, in the love of one equal for another. However disparate (unequal) the other person in material, physical, intellectual or social terms, there is nevertheless a fundamental equality in compassion, a caring *with* another. This is different from *pity* with which it is often confused. Pity stems from a sense of superiority in some aspect of life. We do not feel pity for an equal, so pity is based again in a hierarchical context of those above and those below. Pity does not allow for us to understand how something affects the other. We interpret the other's 'suffering' as we might experience it ourselves, with the risk of being patronising and self-righteous. Compassion, on the other hand, allows us to feel a little of what it's like on the inside of the other person but without needing to invade or losing our separateness. This distinction is similar to that between sympathy *for* and empathy *with* someone.

Self-pity needs to be included here although it is more appropriately placed with angry feelings. Self-pity is the twin of self-blame. It keeps us locked in helplessness and out of touch with our ability to choose and therefore our ability to change.

Happiness could belong in all three polarities: being loved, belonging or being fulfilled. Here it touches on feelings of *joy* and *delight, satisfaction, lightness* and *contentment*. As a transient state, it touches us all: the trap most of us fall into is of equating the feeling of happiness with something we deserve, a public indication of personal validity and success, as if we can be rated by the happiness quotient in our lives. Conversely, this means that *un*happiness is associated with personal failure and inadequacy. This piece of social dogma is powerful enough to persuade us to keep smiling (to indicate happiness) even when, or especially when, this particular feeling has completely disappeared from our current emotional repertoire.

Kites based in the emotions of joy and anger

Livid–explosive–incandescent–simmering–irritated–low–flat–down–feeble–apathetic–listless and high–energetic–buoyant–stretched–charged–powerful are examples of feeling states associated with the engagement/containment polarity.

Guilt is a frequently used relational currency. This feeling derives from an inability to take responsibility for choices, which is embedded in a deeply rooted cultural definition of 'power over' or 'power under' as the only two alternatives. Equality simply does not figure in this picture of relationship; we tend to experience guilt in relation to someone whom we identify as having less power than ourself: less say in the matter, less influence, less voice, less prestige. Guilt is not to be confused with regret, sorrow or sadness that are associated with grief. If you find yourself feeling 'guilty', you could consider whether you are secretly storing some resentment towards the other person or whether what you feel is genuine sorrow.

The equivalent currency of guilt is its opposite: *blame*. This is another kite we frequently use to attempt to express what we are feeling. The associated emotion is some form of anger. Blame is the learned feeling we use to express our sense of powerlessness in relation to someone else, a felt inability to choose, a felt experience of inequality, which fuels a sense of grievance at the injustice. Blame essentially needs an object against which it has to be directed – others or ourselves – and is therefore an aspect of aggression rather than anger.

Disappointment is not to be confused with real sadness. Disappointment often follows failure to match up to an aware or unaware set of expectations (see patterns of anger in Chapter 9) so that disappointment in self or others often masks angry feelings. These are usually expressed indirectly through punitive behaviour or attitudes towards ourselves or the others in question.

Envy is different from jealousy. The accepted distinction between the two is that envy is related to a thing – a quality, material possession or status – whereas jealousy is felt in response to a bond or relationship between two people. Envy is rooted in competitiveness, which is fostered by a comparatively powerless state.

Shame is a deeply learned feeling state, originating early in life. Taking a commonly felt area of shame in our culture – shame about our natural nakedness – it is possible to detect beneath this label a deep rage in response to being looked at, objectified, invaded by look or touch or penetration. Shame incorporates a sense of virginal territory lost, a sense of self and boundary invaded while we are powerless and unable to offer a defence. This feeling is evident in adult women who have experienced the trauma of rape; such a violent invasion can restimulate the earlier feeling of bodily shame, powerlessness and self-blame. This combination of feelings can block the ability to identify and release the appropriate anger that is essential before pride and bodily integrity can be restored. I have found sometimes that beneath shame and rage lies the deeper emotion of grief elicited by that loss of bodily integrity.

Rejection describes another composite feeling, a label that we attach to a variety of feelings and experiences. When we look more closely at the feelings behind the label, we find a measure of hurt with often, behind it, an unexpressed and unacknowledged anger at being ignored, overlooked or unfairly treated in some way. Rejection can become for many of us a feeling in which we get stuck because unless the anger is addressed, the feeling tends to be converted into self-blame. Being rejected then becomes distorted into the belief that the reason for rejection is that we are fundamentally 'rejectable'; this expectation perpetuates itself in self-fulfilling prophesies until the anger can be identified. Once this anger has been released, the hurt can also be acknowledged and the expectation of being rejected can be diminished.

Hurt belongs here because it is much easier for us, especially women, to identify with being upset or hurt when in fact we are completely out of touch with the emotion of anger in our lives. Here the feeling of hurt is a guide to the deeper emotion of anger.

Boredom is a feeling associated with restlessness, irritation and trapped energy. Boredom, like depression, becomes a self-imposed prison, containing the anger that emerges when the need to engage is frustrated. The anger will turn inwards for a while and we switch off and withdraw until the anger pushes for release through an explosion of aggression.

Peace is a surprising feeling to be included here but I think peace, deep true peace does exist within the belly of anger. The balance between self and other, the sense of willing acquiescence, of being met and matched, of yielding to times of real powerlessness – all offer feelings of peace.

Pride, so often associated with arrogance and the consequent fear of downfall, can be a difficult feeling to acknowledge. But pride, in a context of equality, is different. It is associated sometimes with achievement, but also, at heart, it is a celebration of the effort, of the process, of the ability to transcend hardship and difficulty and barriers: a celebration of the commitment to keep going.

Fulfilment belongs here when it means being stretched and challenged and proving adequate to the task, but it can also represent a sense of emotional closeness and love.

Humiliation is similar to shame but is first experienced by most of us at an age when we have had time to absorb and discern the up/down structure of the world in which we live. The experience of humiliation involves loss of face, loss of status, loss of prestige, according to whatever happens to be the current measure of external power. Just under the surface of this feeling is rage, commonly distorted into aggression when the opportunity for revenge presents itself.

Depression is a feeling state that nearly everyone experiences from time to time, associated with feeling disheartened, discouraged, down or despondent. We lose touch temporarily with our capacity for change and feel *defeated* or *overwhelmed* by impossible odds, often indicating the need to take stock, to rest, restore energy levels and find a new strategy or approach. However, depression, in its more severe form, is virtually impossible to describe to anyone who has not experienced it and deserves more space here because it is so open to misunderstanding.

The difference between what people experience at low points in their lives and the more serious illness is an underlying fragility. Some individuals are simply too fragile to survive the ups and downs of life experiences that others, more psychically robust, can weather. Experiences, for example, of redundancy, bullying and harassment, a bereavement or emotional pressure caused by fear of failure can and do prove too much for such an individual to bear.

This underlying fragility is quite evident, even in children. If it is acknowledged along with appropriate and adequate support and education, it is possible for individuals to manage the 'normal' buffeting of life. More often, however, friends, colleagues, teachers, parents and partners do not understand: fearfully and helplessly, they close their eyes to it, often with tragic consequences.

Personal descriptions of depression vary but most include feelings of being imprisoned, trapped, and of suffering acute *despair*. The huge outward-moving energy of anger is turned inwards and trapped. Every bit of physical and mental energy is devoured by the constant, intense psychic pain, sometimes such an inescapable agony that it leads to suicide as the only relief. It is this psychic pain that is hard to comprehend when you're on the outside.

Sometimes, when the pain becomes intolerable, depression shifts to a numb almost *non*-feeling state: you are unable to respond to anyone or anything, all the colour and vitality of life have been sucked into an emotional 'black hole'. When you're in this state of depression, it feels *for ever*. Even though you may have survived a period of depression before and therefore, rationally, know that it may not be permanent, that assurance disappears completely: you are utterly convinced that you are facing eternity.

It is hard to continue with normal interaction. Reluctantly, I once dragged myself, depressed, to attend a conference. Within the confines of a small group discussion, I acknowledged my emotional state. This was immediately leapt upon by another delegate who declared to me, with an exceedingly bright smile, 'Oh, it's *such* a creative time, depression, isn't it?' I remember suppressing a nearly overwhelming desire to slap this woman's face, very hard, and simultaneously feeling grateful that something had triggered an emotion in the bleak and perpetual numbness of life at that time.

Kites based in the emotions of trust and fear

Uncomfortable–ill-at-ease–tense–nervous–jumpy–shocked–excited–on-edge and relaxed–calm–laid-back–steady–open are frequently experienced feeling states associated with the safety/risk polarity.

Anxiety is enabling when it informs us of danger or possible threat, giving us a prompt to be alert and prepared. This is part of the source emotion of fear. Anxiety is also an integral part of any risk – a leap, performance, a task ahead – akin to the feeling of *excitement*. Anxiety becomes a distorted and automatic response when there is no correspondence between stimulus and response. Anxiety then becomes disabling. Instead of informing us of an actual cause for concern that we can then address and in doing so use up the chemicals released in the arousal, this kind of self-perpetuating anxiety fuels itself, getting entangled with previously unreleased fears. Anxious feelings keep whirring round, going nowhere, making us sick or immobilised with their psychosomatic effects.

This kind of learned anxiety can acquire a life of its own; it becomes detached from the source and can develop into a psychosomatic pattern, body feeding mind, mind feeding body. Often, when in this state, it is useful to consider whether we have become stuck simply because of the emotion of anger sitting below the surface. Recognising the deeper emotion can help to break out of the repetitive cycle. Closely allied with this feeling state is *panic*, physiologically similar, and a response to internal fears rather than an appropriate response to an external threat.

Worry is connected to, but need not include, the physical symptoms of anxiety. Worry tends to be experienced through endless thoughts and mental whirrings: we become caught in a cycle of worry like a hamster in a wheel. A social feeling more than an emotion, it is none the less powerful in its compulsion. It is usually connected to fears of getting it wrong, failure or losing control. This means it could be rooted in the emotions of fear or anger, depending on the individual situation.

Loneliness is a composite feeling, different from the actual state of being alone. Feeling lonely can be related to the emotional base of love and grief, a yearning for companionship, to share, and this is often played upon in a culture that promotes the status of 'coupledom' as the only valid state for any adult. It is also a feeling which tells us when we miss the presence of someone dear to us, a temporary or permanent loss.

I've included loneliness here in the base of trust and fear because I believe it often relates more to our need to belong. This applies in a context of home or work or school; it is allied to the feeling of *exclusion* and applies also in a wider context of feeling out of step with everyone else in life, of feeling 'different'.

Confidence can often be misunderstood. Genuine confidence belongs here because it can be rooted in faith and trust in self and/or others. It stems from self-knowledge and a sense of belonging in oneself. The word confidence also is used to describe a feeling that depends less on inner trust and more on a sense of status, achieved by overcoming or suppressing anxiety. The desire to avoid powerlessness encourages us to aim for a confidence based on external power: expertise, getting it right, keeping up appearances. Such confidence is based not on the acknowledgement of anxiety but on an outright denial of its existence.

Stupidity is often mentioned as a feeling. Sometimes we feel stupid when we don't understand something, we can't find the answer or make ourselves understood. This relates feeling 'stupid' to anxiety and fear. Feeling stupid can also be a kite based in the emotion of anger. The label 'stupid' is easily used to put down both ourselves and others and is often related to the perception of powerlessness.

Embarrassment can be part of the range that includes feeling **nervous**, **bashful**, **timid** and **shy** and is related to the fear of not fitting in. Sometimes, though, the feeling of embarrassment describes a loss of face, being exposed and defenceless, a sense of boundaries being transgressed, which would base it in the emotion of anger.

Jealousy is another composite feeling that has different meanings for different people. It can derive from the need to cling on to someone because we fear rejection; it can derive from fear of loneliness. At heart, jealousy seems to be based on fear of abandonment and of being robbed of love or status. It is a powerful learned feeling which can dominate our relationships, fuelling all sorts of actions of revenge; but aggression is usually only the outer response to the unaddressed fear.

Learning a new language

Acknowledging feelings in this way is a vital step in emotional management. It takes time to re-establish a trust in what our bodies are saying to us after years of ignoring or rationalising away our feelings. Once we have started to re-educate our minds not to over-ride our bodies but to work *with* them instead, we will find that identification comes more readily. It really is like learning a new language or relearning a language with the consciousness of an adult. Once we accept everything we find in ourselves, rejecting nothing, we can respond with greater sensitivity and awareness.

The stage of acknowledgement and identification is *for yourself.* It can be enough to acknowledge what we are feeling internally for us to be able to manage our emotional response effectively. On other occasions, we want to communicate: to express these feelings in words to others.

◆ You may be able to devise other kites with feelings that haven't been included here. Work out where you think each belongs: whether it is an emotion or a feeling state and to which emotional base it would be attached.

◆ Are you aware of some feelings that you find it harder to acknowledge than others? If so, give yourself special permission to share these with the person with whom you are doing these exercises.

◆ Remember to practise connecting the acknowledgement of your feeling with your body's sensations.

---

12 | Naming v. Evasion

IN many ways, words are the most difficult medium in which to communicate emotion: expression through colour, form, movement or sound is often easier. Expression in words can be achieved in the form of poetry or fiction but, for most of us, in everyday communication, the linear structure of language distances us from the physical and cyclical nature of emotion. However, it is essential to start finding the basic words of this language.

The most vital tool in managing feelings at this level is **self-disclosure**.

Self-disclosure is not a heart-to-heart dialogue or an opportunity to confess all. It is not fancy, complex, artistic or clever. Self-disclosure is simply taking the internal acknowledgement one stage further: communicating the truth of whatever we are feeling by putting it into words. This description makes it sound so obvious and easy that you may wonder why it should be described as a skill. But having taught this skill over many years, I know, first of all, how supremely effective it is; second, how amazed people are when they get the hang of it because they find it so useful; and, third, how very difficult it is to learn.

The major problem that occurs is in the transition from internal recognition to external expression. For most of our lives, recognition of feeling has been quickly censored, both in our own minds and as far as expression to others is concerned. We have learned to dissemble and hide because expressing feelings means being open and being open is associated with being powerless.

The consequence of this approach is that when we do decide to say how we feel, we tend to defend ourselves against vulnerability by relying on self-righteousness and blame. So the understandable mistake that we make when beginning to use this skill is to *appear* to be expressing our feelings while in reality criticising the other person:

'I feel that you have no right to say that.'
'I feel you shouldn't do that.'
'You make me feel miserable.'

'I feel that you're wrong.'
'You intimidate me.'
'I feel that you're insensitive.'
'You make me feel really small.'

Self-disclosure lies in assuming responsibility for our feelings, which entails recognising that whatever we are feeling cannot be blamed on someone else. This is why it is so difficult to do. It involves a huge shift in awareness: it goes so deeply against the conditioned grain to accept that what we are feeling is what *we* are feeling and that nobody has forced us to feel this way.

Individual responses to perception of another's behaviour vary so much that we cannot simply attribute a feeling to a cause even though we find comfort in doing so. If we take a trivial example of someone treading on your foot, you might argue that you have a case for saying they had caused you pain and that you would be correct in responding with irritation. Even then, though, your response would vary from others' responses to the identical action. You might perceive the action as malicious or accidental; you could be in a good or bad mood when it occurs; maybe you're wearing new shoes; maybe it's happened to you three times before that day; then there's the other person's appearance and manner of response – all these contribute to the way you experience this one action. Your response might therefore be to be outraged, mildly irritated, surprised, even apologetic. The point to remember here is that this skill requires you accustom yourself to stating your experience – your feelings – while suspending the notions of cause or blame.

The skill of self-disclosure lies in being clear and honest and upright.

Being clear. This means being as specific as possible. It improves with practice. At first, we will find that words like 'upset' come more easily than 'angry', that 'confused' hangs around for a while until the fog begins to clear, that we will almost certainly understate the intensity of what we are feeling. Blanket terms of 'rejected' or 'disappointed' or 'guilty' tend to block our ability to be more specific and express ourselves more effectively.

Being honest. There is no point in saying we are 'a bit upset' when we are furious, or 'hurt' when we are angry. Nor is this skill about saying what we think the other person wants to hear! Or what we think might prevent someone expressing anger towards *us*. It is simply about conveying emotional truth as far as we can see it at the time. That is enough.

Being upright. Ultimately, fault and cause and blame become irrelevant. The aim of self-disclosure is to verbalise what we are feeling in response to our perception. Communicating our feelings without blame allows the other person to hear more clearly and the possibility of an *exchange* becomes far more likely.

Self-disclosure is a difficult skill to learn because we are much more accustomed to the route of *evasion*, which we take out of habit and under the influence of the following anxieties:

If I say what I feel, I'll give them more power over me/I'll be more vulnerable/ I'll be labelled hysterical
Although it is true that there are times when it is wiser to keep quiet and more appropriate to do so, self-disclosure enables you to communicate from a position of personal power, not weakness.

I might get it wrong
Fear of looking foolish discourages us from listening to our emotional wisdom and makes us reluctant to address feelings that might put us in a bad light. It also means that we tend to hold back until we imagine we are absolutely in the right and that quickly translates into self-righteousness: an absolute guarantee that the other person will respond defensively.

I can't find the words
Understandable – but practice really does help. The inability to find the words stems from years of denying and ignoring our emotions until they accumulate to a degree when they become unavoidable. We can learn to become more in touch with our feelings from the cues in our bodies, which is where feelings occur, not in our heads.

If I don't say anything, the problem will just go away
Highly unlikely.

Putting feelings into words need not involve blame or apology. Self-disclosure is a way of taking responsibility for what we feel, simply stating the truth, without the need to be right or wrong. We often do get it wrong – we respond to mistaken perceptions – but the only chance we have of sorting out emotional issues in relation to another person is by communicating without blame and more in the spirit of *informing* the other person. We can never make pronouncements with anything approaching absolute certainty. Emotional articulation is relative and, remember, as a medium, emotion is always in motion and is in response to a perception which may be inaccurate or may conflict with someone else's perception. When we state our feelings, we have a chance to compare perceptions and then evaluate our own feelings.

Eventually, feelings can be included as just one part of ordinary communication – as unselfconsciously and as naturally as we communicate our ideas, our opinions or thoughts. Self-disclosure is useful at the actual time of awareness of the feeling or in the longer term, when talking about past events or when wanting, for example, to clarify misunderstandings in any relationship. Apart from opening up the possibility for emotional exchange, this skill also helps to release psychosomatic tension.

Release of tension. Self-disclosure is a vital part of short-term emotional management because it acts as a first and major form of release of tension. This is because until there is an acknowledgement and therefore acceptance of the feeling, whatever it is, the battle will continue between the body, which pushes to release, and the head which has learned to keep everything battened down. The greater the pressure for the feeling to be expressed, the greater the counter-effort of the head to control and prevent expression, the greater the tension, the greater the pressure, and so on. Self-disclosure acts in an extraordinary way to allow the mouth to articulate the feeling, forming a meeting point between the battling head and body: head and body become congruent, acting together instead of against each other, the head finding the language to translate the physical sensations of emotion.

At this point, the conflict eases. There is a felt release of psychosomatic tension, especially if the language conveys the feeling accurately. The arousal doesn't dissipate immediately if it is high, but once the conflict between body and mind stops, once we acknowledge and name the truth of what we are feeling, the struggle subsides and the tension becomes more manageable. It is as if by signalling to our psyches that we have taken note of what is occurring, that our bodies no longer need to keep turning up the volume to penetrate the obtuseness of our minds.

The limits of self disclosure. With the practice of self-disclosure, we become aware of the reality of restimulation. This is because once we stop holding others accountable for making us feel whatever we feel; once we state the truth of what we experience; once we take the risk of exchanging this information instead of letting everything fester inside our heads, we discover that our own perceptions are different. We discover that what we see or what we hear may have something to do with reality but also that our response is often completely out of proportion.

If we are honest enough with ourselves, we realise that what we feel is more to do with what we carry around within ourselves in our personal emotional ragbags. We see that unexpressed and unreleased feelings from the past are responsible for restimulating our emotions in the present. My own belief is that these unresolved emotions unconsciously move us towards situations and relationships and involvements with other people as an opportunity to *resolve* whatever items in our ragbags are ready for processing and sorting.

The 'magnetic impulse' that draws two individuals together always seems miraculous to me. Such relationships are often portrayed on screen or in literature. The Brazilian film *Central Station* is a wonderful example of such a relationship between a middle-aged woman, Dora, and a young boy, Josué. It begins when his mother is killed in an accident. While helping him to find his father, Dora relives her own childhood experience of her relationship with her drunken father after her mother's early death and her involvement with Josué acts as a catalyst for emotional change in her.

Sometimes these relationships appear in an intimate context, sometimes in a professional or family context. Lasting for years or only for days, they provide us with an opportunity of working something through. Many of us are familiar with the idea of this when we wake up to find we've married our mothers (or fathers) or when we meet someone who disturbs us by mirroring a little too closely something in our selves we would prefer to ignore.

Restimulation, in itself, stirs up or brings to the surface emotions that have been frozen for all the reasons we've looked at in previous chapters. How do we know when we are restimulated?

Apart from the clue of disproportion described in Chapter 8 there is another telltale clue: with practice, we can discern a childlike quality to our feelings. We feel somehow very small and either extremely powerless, pathetic and defenceless or, on the other hand, tyrannical, monstrous and capable of terrible destruction. This emerges in non-verbal cues such as tone of voice or gesture, manner of crying or stamping the foot – a childish exaggeration in our emotional behaviour.

As always with this topic, it isn't possible to make a rigid demarcation between a stimulus that is real and happening *now* and the effect of unreleased and accumulated feelings from the *past*. All you can do is begin to develop a familiarity with your own emotional responses so that you will recognise when you are responding disproportionately, as in the following examples of restimulation.

Imagine feeling a wave of irritation towards a particularly trying pupil or your stomach sinking as you prepare to enter the office of an overbearing and 'difficult' supervisor. Imagine wanting to scream with exasperation at the tenth demand from your small child or feeling your throat contract as you see the pain in the face of the elderly man listening while you explain that his wife is soon going to die. Imagine arriving home tired to find your family's unwashed supper dishes and wanting to explode.

The trying pupil is no doubt very trying in reality: so what gets in the way of your ability to be patient and firm and caring? The unpleasant supervisor would realistically warrant a cautious approach, but not feelings of dread and powerlessness. What is it that can make you almost murderous towards your demanding child instead of being able to deflect the real and unimagined irritation? And when you care for the people you deal with and it is part of your job to deliver sad tidings, how does it happen that on this occasion you find yourself overcome with emotion? How does the exasperation at finding chores not done acquire the significance of a personal affront and a blatant confirmation of your menial status?

The short answer to all these questions is restimulation: the long answers are impossibly varied. Hypothetically, there could be hundreds of strands, depending on past experience, but what keeps the restimulation operative is the unreleased and therefore unaware emotional fallout from these past experiences, whatever they are.

So, if you can identify what you feel and then recognise that it is, in some way, disproportionate, childish or an over-reaction, you will know that you are restimulated. What can you do about this?

First, you can acknowledge this fact to yourself and take the time to reflect. In the light of this awareness of past influences, you can reassess your present situation. It may be enough to know that you are bringing much more to the situation than it warrants – that perhaps you are reading something in it that isn't there – for you to alter your approach and behaviour. It gives you the possibility of choice.

Second, especially if the relationship is important to you, you can communicate this awareness so that the other person doesn't feel responsible for the intensity of your emotional response. With practice, you can discern more and more readily the quality of restimulated, exaggerated, childish emotion in yourself and, in this way, you can choose not to act out. (Acting out describes using past feelings for emotional fuel, leading to some of the patterns already described in Chapter 9.) To stop doing this, you don't need to know the exact nature of the connections with the past entanglements. You need only an awareness, not an analysis, and since emotion will cloud your rational self anyway, it is a waste of time trying to analyse.

To a certain extent, thinking and therefore making cognitive connections with past experience can be enough to avoid acting out. What usually happens, though, is that at some point, the arousal of emotion – a confusing tangle of recent past, long ago past and present – will break through in some way. If you want to take a further step, you have a third option.

This brings us to the next stage of emotional management. It concerns the aspect of emotional release that cannot be achieved through words – it is, in fact, what happens when the words *stop*.

◆ Take turns with your partner in these exercises to share experiences of restimulated feeling.

◆ Are there relationships in your past or current life which have a quality of restimulated emotion? E.g. experiencing yourself excessively drawn to someone, or frightened, or intimidated, or intolerant?

---

13 | Catharsis v. Accumulation

IT is at this point that most of us feel as if we are peering over the edge of an almighty abyss. Talk *about* feelings? I can manage that. Express *my* feelings? With a bit of practice, perhaps I could learn to do that. *Release* feelings? Never!

The inhibitions that many of us experience stand in stark contrast to the immediate and uncluttered emotional release and expression of childhood. Clearly, we cannot go back. It would not be appropriate to do so. That kind of naive release belongs to childhood where there are few preconceptions and little or no backlog. Release in very young children can be traced to one specific stimulus: a lost toy, a bruised knee, a reprimand, a frightening noise, a refusal. This triggers a response, which prompts arousal and psychosomatic release in a cycle that is quickly over.

Complete release in adults is very different. It is not display or tantrum or 'childish' behaviour. It is not indiscriminate or uncontrollable regression. Emotional release in adulthood is also a different experience because of the passage of time. The simple and straightforward release of childhood evolves over the years into a complex and convoluted process.

Adult release differs from childhood release in two major ways: first, it means making a *choice* to trust and go with your body, and second there is the component of *insight*.

The combination of choice and insight elevates childhood release into adult catharsis.

Catharsis is a blend of the kinds of physiological release described in Chapter 7 plus psychological insight.

Physiological release. This is exactly what it sounds like: release through the various bodily systems of stored up emotional and physical tension. This includes trembling, crying, shaking, groaning, sobbing, shouting, growling, making sounds which cannot be described accurately in words, sweating, screaming. Remember that each primary emotion has its own rhythm and form of release and its own energy so the dynamic of authentic catharsis reflects these different and changing patterns.

Catharsis requires a decision to trust your body to be carried on the ebbs and flows of emotion. Although initial lack of familiarity can be balanced by a developing self-trust, the tendency towards the mind–body division, to impose mind over matter through intellectualisation, will always need to be challenged. We do not need so much to learn the facility of physical release because it is innate, but we have temporarily to suspend automatic physical and mental defences and rigidity. For catharsis, we need to learn the language of emotion *through the body* instead of through the head alone.

Physiological release is essential to the process because it is only when we can learn to trust our bodies that we can stop battling with the brain. The effect of our conditioning is permanent: the mental patterns are ingrained for ever. What we can do, however, is circumvent the brain. We can subvert it, bypass it in different ways by focusing on the body. This involves a clear choice: to stay with, to allow, to trust a process which, at every opportunity, will be subject to 'the static interference' of mental conditioning.

By the time an adult decides to relearn these skills, she/he will have accumulated a psychic and somatic backlog of unexpressed emotion ranging across the years which results in entrenched patterns, some lightly etched, some deeply engraved. Adult catharsis assumes the form of travelling through an extraordinary and individual labyrinth, composed of memories, images, associations and every range of emotion in varying shades of intensity. The labyrinth contains areas quite beyond conscious reach, probably unknowable in that person's lifetime, along with other more accessible parts which can be safely and usefully explored, though always via circuitous routes.

As we learn to relax and allow the process of release to occur, as we begin to retrain our bodies to go *with* instead of *against* release, we find that emotions have a course of their own. Fear triggers rage or grief which bumps into a feeling or memory of being deeply loved; love switches to anxiety which touches an image arousing laughter, then anger, and so on: just as one event in our lives can trigger all kinds of emotion, so release involves a sequence of feelings in response to any particular aspect of our experience.

An important and influential past relationship or event may be revisited again and again and feelings may recur with varying degrees of intensity. Revisiting can happen many times: such is the sensitivity of this psychosomatic mechanism that nothing emerges before it is ready to be acknowledged and released. The process of catharsis is not open to rationalisation: it cannot be subjected to rules and laws and deadlines. You need to suspend your intellect for a while and *trust* that what emerges is appropriate even if it catches you unawares.

Because catharsis is not subject to rational laws, it is not possible to decide what you are going to revisit. You can aim yourself in a certain direction, but as likely as not you will end up down another path addressing something that is more available for release and often, with hindsight, at the root of what you *thought* was going on.

Allowing release to occur naturally will entail emptying a series of 'pockets'. This describes how I have always seen the process working. When someone is in catharsis, they are emptying out a little or large pocket of stored-up emotion. With time and experience, you can recognise when each pocket is empty, in much the same way as knowing when you have vomited up all that needed to be emptied from your stomach.

Emptying a pocket does not mean that the entire matter or relationship has been sorted out, beaten, analysed, dealt with for ever. It simply means that the amount that was available for release has been released. It may be a short time or a long time, or never, before emotions relevant to that particular part of your heartscape come to the fore again. You simply cannot predict: just ride the current of the moment.

Catharsis is a skill in emotional management that stands in stark contrast to the prevailing tendency towards **accumulation**. Catharsis entails relearning how to go *with* your body; accumulation results from struggling *against* your body. We have looked at how accumulated and blocked emotion leads to the establishment of patterns (Chapter 9). The locked emotional energy shows itself in the ways we tend to 'act out' our feelings upon others. We find ourselves responding to situations and relationships with so much restimulated emotion that we lose touch with our inner emotional balance. The more unbalanced we become, the more extreme our behaviour, the more distorted our perceptions become and the less able we are to take emotional responsibility for anything.

We may have a dim but frightening awareness of the struggle with rising levels of fear or rage or pain. We notice possible signs of agitation: numbness and withdrawal; hysteria; feeling frayed or fragmented; obsessive thoughts; suicidal or murderous preoccupations. We may be surprised by unpredictable and inexplicable behaviour: tears welling up for no apparent reason; slips of the tongue, snide comments, something snaps and we let fly; bursting into tears behind a closed door.

We may recognise feeling 'driven' or compelled to some activity, such as eating, drinking, shopping or criticising someone. When the pressure is high, it can feel as if we are on a merry-go-round. We can feel lost, caved in, absent, as if we are looking at life through a telescope, an outside observer rather than a participant.

This escalation will continue until it reaches a breaking point that varies from person to person. The pressure may result in an avalanche of aggression. We lash out indiscriminately at others who may have behaved in a way that triggers release. At the precise moment of avalanche though, we are not too bothered about fairness because we so desperately need to release the pressure and pain inside us.

Sometimes instead of exploding outwards, the rumbles result in subsidence: we collapse under the strain of it all, we go to bed, our back gives way, our immune system breaks down, we succumb to a latent virus. Whether the subsidence is physical or psychological, or both, depends on personal susceptibilities. The consequences can range from three weeks in bed to an incapacitating illness lasting several years; from prolonged outbursts of sobbing through depression, to the experience of a complete nervous breakdown.

Whether mounting pressure results in explosion or implosion, it is important to realise that some release occurs. It may be messy, confused, chaotic and socially unacceptable but, under extreme pressure, a 'window' of release appears in the normally highly-guarded walls of our mind–body defences.

This is a way we survive psychosomatically but, without making connections and releasing some of the past emotion, resolution will not be possible. Although *something* emerges and, psychosomatically, things are set in motion, we then tend to batten down the hatches.

In between and going nowhere. This brings us to one of the most familiar features of the consequences of accumulation instead of catharsis: the point at which we find ourselves caught in a battle between mind and body. It usually occurs when some unwelcome emotion has begun to be released, for whatever reason. We may start to cry and then stop, for all sorts of 'reasons'. For the rest of the day and maybe the next, our eyes are puffy, we get headaches and are unable to function properly. Or in the aftermath of an aggressive outburst, we feel remorseful for the over-reaction and possible hurt and embarrassment caused and try hard to rationalise away our feelings.

If there is a lot pressing for release, this phase lasts for a while. We usually feel miserable, quite appropriately so, because it *is* a miserable place in which to be stuck. We are trapped between two preferable options: behind is the place of the head, firmly in control with the lid tightly on; ahead is the place of psychosomatic, mind–body co-operation, allowing the emotion to be *fully* released. In between is this awful middle ground, where the body is still battling with the brain. The body urges release: it is time to let go of something; the brain responds with images, thoughts, and messages of warning: all manifestations of fear. The latter appear in the following guises:

'How embarrassing!'
'I'm too tired.'
'I've done nothing but cry for days.'
'I'm *sick* of crying.'
'I haven't got the strength.'
'It's pointless.'
'There really isn't anything wrong.'
'It is just self-indulgent.'
'All I do is feel sorry for myself.'
'I've got to snap out of it/pull myself together.'
'I can take a look at these problems when I've finished the term/the project/passed my exams/the children are coping better/I've more time/ after the audition.'
'It's just my hormones/that time of the month.'

This kind of mental censorship also acts at a less conscious level. Even if a significant component of her emotional build-up is anger, a woman may find herself unable to admit to the existence of this particular emotion in her own emotional repertoire and is therefore only able to release tears, which may help a little but not provide complete release. For similar reasons, a man may be able to relieve tension only through aggressive outbursts and remain unable to touch the deeper components of anxiety and fear, simply because he has learned to deny the existence of these feelings. Release cannot be complete because no amount of aggression will *release* fear – it just keeps it at bay.

The brain weighs us down with an impossible clutter of ratio-nalised and acquired fears. What compounds this awful state is that it feels painful – because it *is*. The battle between brain and body, both voluntary and involuntary, the pain in our heads, behind the eyes, in the jaw, in the chest, shoulders, down the spine, in the diaphragm, is real. It is the upper body that bears the brunt of this battle, a tug-of-war between head and gut.

Because of the very real pain and discomfort, we attribute this to the actual emotion. This is why feelings get a bad name because we have come to believe that emotion hurts. The truth is that it is the conflict that hurts; it is the conflict that causes the pain physically. *Release does not hurt*. It is when we go against the body that we feel this pain, not when we go with it. Since most adults never experience psychosomatic release, they never have the opportunity to discover this for themselves.

This in-between stage can become prolonged: we get stuck in repetitive bouts of crying or tantrums or cycles of anxiety, getting nowhere. Furthermore, because of our confusion, we associate tears with being in pain, both in ourselves and others, which is why this 'stuck', purgatorial place is also characterised by the quest for sympathy.

The quest for sympathy. We feel sorry for ourselves and want others to notice and feel sorry for us. We associate being emotional with being childish. We feel unhappy, needy, in trouble and this evokes a wish to be comforted, to be kissed better, made happy. So part and parcel of this stuck state is a need to be noticed and rescued.

The quest for sympathy can last for a long time. It tends not to achieve its goal after a while, partly because others may try and comfort us, believing we are in pain, but then feel helpless or irritated with the never-changing status quo. In addition, however much comfort we receive, the underlying battle is still there – it can be resolved only if and when we face the anxiety of going deeper and moving through it. Until that happens we can go on and on, talking about things, feeling sorry for ourselves, expressing the need for help, and meaning it to some extent, but, underneath, the fear of losing control retains its hold.

Shut-down. When the tremors, the eruptions and the occasions of subsidence are only minor we recover more quickly, but there is usually little awareness of how things built up in the way they did. Even when we reach crisis point, we do not know how collapse could have been avoided or the nature of the actual emotions involved. Although we put our best efforts into recovery, sometimes with the help of professionals, the links between the body and mind remain elusive. Our lack of comprehension serves only to reinforce our resolve to button up more than ever and to remain wary of any emotion.

This can persuade us to suppress feelings even more rigorously. In order to prevent arousal even beginning to make itself felt, we shut off from people and the possibility of responding. We settle at a point of neutrality, conserving emotional energy for those in our immediate circle; sometimes we avoid closeness and intimacy altogether.

We discover that our ability to respond emotionally to joyous events becomes muted as well. We find ourselves wishing we could feel more passion and warmth and celebration in response to our loves and lives. Although we struggle more consciously to suppress what we perceive as negative and therefore unwelcome feelings, keeping the lid on arousal means keeping the lid on *everything*.

♦ Look again at the description of avalanche and subsidence on page 132 and see if you recognise occasions of these in your life. Can you now identify what needs were being blocked and the consequent emotions? Try and recognise the connection between a build-up of emotional tension and the eventual outcome.

♦ Have you ever found yourself feeling stuck in an emotional mess and unable to get further in or get properly out? Has this made you wary of exploring emotion? Did you seek help from someone outside? Was this help effective?

---

14 | Evaluation v. Distortion

Remember that catharsis is a mind–body release. After authentic and complete catharsis, we experience an awareness of physiological release. This is felt as increased physical energy or as a deep stillness. We feel a sense of vitality and well-being, a feeling of coming back into our body-self. Once the muscular tension has been released, there may also be temporary exhaustion. Overall there is a feeling of restoration and balance.

As catharsis is a release of psychic as well as somatic tension, there is a second essential dimension, which makes it deeper and more complete than physical release alone. As I mentioned in the previous chapter, what transforms the simpler process of childhood release into adult catharsis is the potential for insight.

Sometimes, the circumstances allow a release that is very, very deep, at other times, less so. But whenever release has been adequate, when a pocket of emotion has been emptied, the person will spontaneously experience an **insight**, literally, 'a seeing within', an inner understanding. This may be a major illumination or a minor confirmation, it may be immediate or follow within hours, but what is essential is that it comes from inside. This means that, unlike the very best and most correct advice from the outside, you hear or see something at precisely the moment you are ready for it. In this way, you use it and incorporate the information into your current attitudes, behaviour and relationships.

The insight is made possible through the liberation of trapped emotion: a psychological release that allows the *seeing of what could not be seen before*. What blocked the view was the frozen, unreleased emotion: the energy keeping in place the stored, remembered images, sensations and perceptions. It is such a perplexing tangle that I imagine an average adult psyche as thousands of tiny, inter-weaving, different-coloured wires presenting an utterly baffling picture in its intricacy and apparently impenetrable complexity. And yet, there is a sequence underlying the complexity. The apparent chaos of our psyches, in terms of neurophysiological structures that link different regions of the brain with the rest of our bodies, also has an *experiential* order although it defies complete human understanding.

It is easier to glimpse this experiential order through catharsis: seeing and experiencing the complexity through the process of unravelling tiny sections. True and complete catharsis is an extraordinary and inspiring sequence of events. Sometimes insights come in a flood, either straight away or after the body and psyche have become quiescent; sometimes we experience a great 'Aha!' out of the blue.

Evaluation

This is the final stage of the DANCE approach. Evaluation of your emotional response to a given situation requires clarity. With the familiarity of our heartscape that comes primarily through catharsis, we can recognise what happens to restimulate us, the stimuli that hold for us the potential, in some way, for a distorted and disproportionate response. In addition, when events catch us unawares, which they usually do, it takes less time to recognise that we are restimulated or that there is something blocking perception even if we don't know exactly what it is. If this is the case, we can choose to use the skills of catharsis in order to understand more clearly what cannot be seen while our heads are too muddied with stirred up and unresolved distress.

Insight can take the form of remembering an incident from the past that has triggered an over-reaction in the present. This enables us to adjust our perceptions accordingly. Insight may involve a broader reference to a personal pattern of behaviour such as overeating or always settling for second best or an inability to be intimate. In this instance, insight might be a realisation of the emotional origins of this behaviour, giving us an opportunity to evaluate our feelings in a new light.

Insight could enable you to bring into conscious sight a connection between problems you are having with your boss and your past experience with a particular school teacher; or make you aware that your reluctance to take the initiative stems from a deep anxiety dating from your early years. It could help you see that the ongoing difficulty with your teenaged son and your irritation with him is, in fact, a defence against much deeper feelings of loss and sadness at his imminent departure from home. Each of these insights offer an opportunity to evaluate your feelings and to adjust your emotional response and communication as a consequence.

Occasionally an insight can reflect on the universe at large: a discovery about the universality of love, perhaps, or the true nature of beauty. Whether cosmic or prosaic, an insight offers the chance for evaluation of our feelings, our responses and our relationships in a new light. We can then decide how to manage our feelings differently and what step to take next.

In some circumstances, it may be enough to acknowledge our feelings without anyone else being involved. Realising we are restimulated allows us to leave the room and cool down in private before behaving in a way we might regret.

With practice, even when we are clouded by emotion, we can bypass *Catharsis* and go from *Naming* to *Evaluation*, once we become more adept at recognising the signs of distortion and arousal. An insight, once gained in this way, will have a lasting effect and help us evaluate what we feel on the spot, enabling us to choose how to manage our feelings and express ourselves appropriately.

Evaluating feelings of envy, for example, can help you to see how you might improve aspects of your own life. Perhaps you too could get a mortgage, start a course of study, take a long overdue holiday, express yourself more creatively – in other words, redirect the energy of envy into your own life in some concrete way.

You can choose to communicate your feelings with words, directly, as in self-disclosure, when you recognise the need to inform someone of a difficulty or misunderstanding in a relationship. Using your insight into a situation, you can choose to communicate your feelings indirectly: a resolution to change a behaviour pattern could entail buying flowers for someone special, becoming more affectionate, setting clearer limits.

We can choose to communicate our feelings through a form of creative expression. This might be through the use of colour, fabric, poetry, clay, music, dance – any medium that allows personal expression of what we feel.

All these methods of communication allow for some release; other means of physical and mental release already mentioned will also offer some temporary release. However, without ever experiencing the complete psychosomatic release of catharsis, as proposed in this approach, the unreleased emotion will remain fully or partially a potential for distortion.

Distortion

Distortion is the prevailing alternative to evaluation. It is evident in our communication with others in the ways we seek to blame or target them with the oppression we have ourselves suffered. It is evident in the ways we fear and mistrust others; in the ways we compare and compete with others; in the way we regard love as a scarce commodity to be hoarded; or in the ways we treat ourselves, and others, as objects.

Distortion causes us to lavish on a child the love we didn't experience ourselves, without due regard for the child as a separate individual. Distortion is tragically evident in the repetitive cycle of abuse that the abused hand on when they themselves are in a position of some power. When suppressed emotions are restimulated and emerge psychosomatically, they are ready to be dealt with, to be expressed and released. Instead of being able to see this for what it is, an opportunity to heal past experiences by releasing the emotions that keep us locked in our patterns, distortion leads to blame, over-reaction, a confusion of present and past emotion, with consequences ranging from merely unfortunate to fatal. And we are usually none the wiser for it.

Distortion is also evident in our continuing fear and mistrust of our bodies so that even if we learn a little of the language of emotion, it remains an intellectual experience. Without catharsis, we are still able to subject emotion to rational control by ensuring that feelings remain verbal entities so that we never experience the language of emotion *beyond words*.

Emotion as energy

Living the mind–body link emotionally is, I believe, vital. This means that catharsis has to be included in any healthy approach to emotional management. As anyone who has experienced it will testify, the psychosomatic energy released when blocked emotion is cleared is extraordinary. When it is trapped, it distorts and saps us at every level of our being. Once released as just so much 'stuff', we can get on with our lives more fully. Sometimes this can be felt as a renewal of loving or increased determination to find a way through a particular problem. We feel more joy and empowerment. Instead of being trapped and festering, the energy becomes a fuel for creative use. Fear can be felt as excitement or we can experience a deep, deep sense of peace.

The aim is not to achieve an emotionless state – it is not a question of getting to the bottom once and for all – where the past is healed for ever. Even with the release of catharsis, the deepest layers of grief and anger and fear do not disappear altogether. One of the conventions which arises from confusion about emotion is that 'time heals'. Anyone who has suffered a loss of a much beloved other, anyone who has suffered terribly from cruelty and injustice, will know that this is a nonsense. Time covers wounds with distance but it doesn't heal: psychosomatic release heals, not entirely, but adequately and more thoroughly than anything else I know.

Once enough of the stored grief, anger and fear from the past has been processed sufficiently, we can use the released energy in a different way. I have already mentioned that revisiting sites of past pain and trauma can happen many times over. But there comes a time when we have released enough to let go of blame of self and others. We have enough insight and familiarity to navigate our personal heartscape and avoid the eddies of life-restricting behaviour in order to use the substance of emotional energy in a different form.

This can be a direct use of energy for change at a personal or global level. Once anger has been processed, it becomes a remarkable force for campaigning and espousing causes devoted to challenging and redressing some of the injustices in the world. Transformed fear can be a force of courage and connection with others, generating the sturdiness of heart to withstand isolation.

Once personal grief has been processed sufficiently, it can enable us to open our hearts much more fully to others, to experience a much wider dimension of love than one that is restricted to only a few individuals in a lifetime. It becomes transformed into energy that we can use, in a professional or personal context, to help the healing process of all kinds of wounds in others.

Distorted (because frozen) emotional energy spawns a host of distortions in behaviour, thinking, attitudes and perceptions at a personal level. Individual patterns have been described in Chapter 9 but this distorted energy extends from the personal to social and cultural attitudes and behaviour. It would be truer to say that restimulation, not love, makes the world go round.

Taking responsibility for what we are feeling and using the insight that comes from catharsis allow us to evaluate and illuminate our behaviour and responses. The energy of emotion when harnessed in this way is a force for potential transformation, individually and collectively.

Allowing restimulation to rule our behaviour instead, with all its terrifying distortions and misperceptions, lets the energy run amuck. Instead of being guided by light, it becomes a force of darkness. Because the energy remains without the light of insight, it does untold harm at an unconscious level – individual upon individual, nation upon nation – and the wounds, as long as they remain unidentified, can never be healed.

Part Three

THE MIND–BODY LINK
IN EVERYDAY LIFE

IN this book, I have tried to convey the importance of emotion: its relevance, its nature, its potential for being a positive or distorted force in our lives. I have emphasised the necessity of educating children about emotions, in the same way we teach them about basic biology at school, in order to learn how to manage feelings appropriately using the DANCE approach.

I have tried to write in such a way that the reader could receive the information with head and heart combined. All of this, by necessity, has been in words. The stages of the DANCE approach – Distress, Acknowledgement, Naming, Catharsis and Evaluation – are easy to understand in words. Possibly much of the content of this book has been interesting in terms of understanding more about where feelings come from and why we have them.

Intellectual understanding is a very helpful start. Understanding that feelings arise in healthy response to our needs being met or unmet can allow us to be more accepting of what we are feeling and perhaps address the particular need. Once we decide to acknowledge we do have an emotional life, we become more aware of what is going on.

We can choose to express what we are feeling to someone else, either for general support or to clarify and work through a difficulty. If we realise we are in a 'mood', it can be guaranteed that restimulated feelings are around. This information can help us choose to handle a situation differently. We can learn to monitor our own levels of arousal, by becoming familiar with our responses and spotting danger signs – such as drinking a little too much alcohol or collecting grievances or fantasies spinning round in our heads.

We can also be more open to others, allowing and encouraging them to express feelings they might not otherwise be able to. Including feelings on the agenda with work or family or friends is a huge and vital aspect of healthy relationships.

However, all the way through the book, I have emphasised the psychosomatic nature of emotion and it is the necessity of referring to the body that we resist. However much we agree with the concept, it is harder to put into practice because it flies in the face of generations of conditioning.

Noticing the body's responses and identifying that something is out of balance (Distress), and releasing accumulated emotion as an integral part of physical or mental health (Catharsis), require something beyond words; these skills require a degree of awareness of and trust in the body that is beyond the reach of most adults.

Whenever I teach management of feelings or work with individuals, the biggest stumbling block is the stage of catharsis. Why is this? What are we so afraid of? First, we're afraid of losing control: what is above the neck is controllable – what is below appears unfathomable. We imagine that once we have loosened the controls that there is only a very, very long way down and no way up again. Sometimes, this fantasy is partly based on past experience of 'getting emotional' and recollections of a prolonged and messy episode.

The fear is also sourced in deeper levels of fantasy, so deeply embedded that they are scarcely conscious. These fantasies have assumed those exaggerated qualities of infant experience described in Chapter 4: images and associations of disappearing, chaos, mess, awful pain, even suffocation and disintegration. These sorts of fantasies influence many adults' conscious resistance to losing control emotionally although we allow ourselves to do so in other contexts.

We choose in a sexual context, for example, or while practising some forms of meditation, to suspend our minds and temporarily give over the 'rule' to the body. Although anxiety prevents some individuals from suspending the mind during sexual activity with the result that they stay more rational and more in control, becoming more mechanical in their behaviour, this is not the norm. However, it *is* considered normal to inhibit the experience of emotional arousal. Whereas sexual release – in prescribed contexts – is encouraged and endorsed, emotional release is not. The combination of habitual inhibition and the immense, almost unbreakable command of the head and all our cognitive learning will ensure that we stay in control.

This accounts for the prevalence of therapy and counselling which is word-based. Feelings will be described, considered, challenged and occasionally released in the form of naming and self-disclosure. Occasional physical release may be seen as acceptable, but never vital. I believe it is vital – essential for life – because without ever experiencing complete psychosomatic release, our system breaks down. The psychic or somatic mechanism becomes impaired. The next two chapters describe the repercussions of lack of catharsis on our mental health and our physical health.

15 | How emotions affect the mind

SINCE the experience of emotion occurs in the body *and* mind, our capacity to think is inextricably linked with emotion. Those infallible paths of reason and logic are, in fact, prone to constant and permanent distortion because of the psychosomatic effects of conscious and unconscious emotional arousal.

Distortion leads to the first aspect of mental impoverishment: namely, the inability to think clearly. We are all familiar with the impossibility of being able to 'think straight' when under pressure, feeling nervous, agitated, shocked or extremely sad. In other words, reason and high emotion tend not to be able to function simultaneously. We simply cannot be rational when under the influence of high levels of emotion. This applies to the impossibility of communicating effectively (i.e. so that the other person can hear) when we are steaming with anger. It also explains why we cannot learn – take in information – when we are upset or embarrassed or frightened of failure. This is because the chemicals produced by these feelings get in the way. Our heads do not function properly when we are overwhelmed or moved: the aroused emotions (including restimulated emotions) trigger a mass of chemical change in our bodies that interferes with our intellectual capacity for clear, logical, unmuddied *thought*. This phenomenon accounts for a huge percentage of 'low achievement' among schoolchildren. Anxiety is the single most effective way of killing any possibility of real learning in children and adults alike: none of us can learn when we are not feeling safe enough to make mistakes.

The effect of current emotion on learning – the emotional response to the actual situation – is one dimension of distortion. Our intellectual clarity is further impeded by the backlog of restimulated emotion elicited by conscious and unconscious memories, associations and images all held tightly in frozen emotional blocks.

In Chapter 9, we looked at patterns of behaviour and the role of cognitive or mental patterns. The hub of the wheel represents the emotional core; the wheelband, the actual behaviour patterns and the spokes keeping the two together represent the cognitive patterns. These are thoughts, messages, images, assumptions about ourselves, others, life in general and our particular place in the scheme of things. They exert a powerful influence because we think, we anticipate, we fantasise along the lines prescribed by these messages. They provide a constant connection to the unexpressed and frozen emotional core, which is where they come from, and keep us bound to behave in particular ways to reinforce them.

Examples of cognitive patterns follow in three groups related to the three polarities.

From a core of trapped grief (and love):

'People always hurt you in the end.'
Nobody wants to know you if you're sad.'
'If they knew the real me, they'd be repelled.'
'They'll never know how much I've done for them.'
'She/he is bound to leave me eventually.'
'I don't need anyone – I'm better off on my own.'
'I am useless/bad/worthless/rubbish.'

From a core of trapped anger (and joy):

'Get him first.'
'An eye for an eye.'
'He deserves to be punished.'
'Always look out for Number One.'
'Show them who's boss.'
'Dog eat dog.'
'Winner takes all.'
'Smash/thump/finish/ annihilate them!'
'It's utterly hopeless.'
'I'm a complete failure.'
'I've nobody to blame but myself.'

In addition, the unexpressed anger becomes internalised in the form of a hidden but powerful set of *shoulds*: how I should appear, how I should be behaving, how my life should be going, what kind of mother I should be. This applies with equal severity to the others in our lives: what kind of parent he should have been, the kind of relationship we should be having, the kind of wife I should have

the right to expect. These prescriptions interfere with real engagement because comparison distorts our perception and, against this
constant barrage of criticism, it is impossible to develop a real
appreciation of one's self or others.

Finally, from a core of trapped fear (and trust):

'Always watch your back.'
'The world is an unsafe place.'
'Never trust strangers.'
'Don't let anyone see you too closely.'
'It's safer not to ask questions.'
'Don't rock the boat.'
'Ignorance is bliss.'
'Keep foreigners out.'
'Pretend you know what you're doing.'

If you recognise any of these ways of thinking as your own, you
will see how these faulty mental patterns dominate lives, restrict
behaviour and govern expectations of relationships.

The problem is exacerbated by our inability to recognise
when our clarity has disappeared. We have been so steeped in anti-
emotional conditioning that fear and lack of information persuade
us to control and deny what we are feeling and to maintain a
semblance of rational dignity come what may. It is very much the
norm to make authoritative and self-righteous pronouncements –
on personal, social and political topics – based on emotionally
charged and distorted perceptions, under the persuasive and potent
guise of reason and logic.

From this point, it is only a short step to see how these ways of
thinking have become the bases for the rules and regulations of
social behaviour. The establishment of what is upheld as 'normal'
and the cultural legacy described in Chapter 1 have been enshrined
in all our institutions: educational, medical, legal, religious, political, commercial. This explains why we continue to promote the
belief that the head knows best. It is also why I believe the only hope
for a change in attitudes to emotion is to include information about
its process and management in general education. At least then,
perhaps, it would be possible for more children to grow up without
needing to continue the cycle of restimulation and suppression (and
oppression) when they, in turn, become adults.

Fear of emotion has contributed to intellectual impoverishment with its effect on our capacities for imagining, for choosing and for knowing.

Imagination. Imagination requires an openness and lack of fear, a readiness to risk going beyond the known and familiar. When our capacity to trust becomes restricted we are unable to withstand fear and so we cannot truly imagine. Imagining means being able to break through the bonds of limiting rationalism and to savour everything without judgement. It entails going beyond the given, moving through realms of doubt and uncertainty, suspending the safety of dogmatism, approval and the need to belong. Imagination is a valuable creative potential in each of us which is all too often stifled by adherence to a linear tradition and rigid ideals.

Imagination requires sensitivity and emotional sensitivity is one aspect. Emotion can block or nourish imagination. Too much restimulation inhibits imagination through fear. It can also hamper the creative expression of what we imagine. If the emotion is too crude and unprocessed, it hampers clarity – the words, the forms, are communicated along with the unprocessed emotion. This often causes in the listener or reader, at a subconscious level, an interference with what the artist is attempting to communicate – like static on a radio or television transmission. The substance of emotion needs to be refined enough through release and insight to be used in a purer form if needed to communicate. At this point, transformed and transmuted, it can be used to inform, enhance and intensify the expression, so as to move others at a deeper level.

Choice. The ability to choose how to behave is a human refinement, distinguishing us from many animals. Unfortunately, many of us do not exercise choice because we cannot take responsibility for our emotions. The prerequisite for conscious choice is responsibility.

The man who understands that his 'anger' is triggered by a mixture of fears – past, present, real and imaginary – and who learns to recognise signals of arousal can then make an informed personal choice to behave differently. The woman who has recovered enough of her sense of personal power, through releasing her rage at an experience of violation, can leave behind the helplessness of victim status and choose how she wants to proceed with her life.

As long as the energy continues to revolve around blame and

fault and as long as we feel at the mercy of emotion, we cannot make an informed choice.

Knowing. Intellectual comprehension is vital: we need our minds and our reason and all our rational faculties to learn and develop and acquire information. However, exclusive dependence on what can be scientifically proved or what would be upheld in a court of law leaves us without the advantage of 'emotional intelligence'. In my book *A Woman In Your Own Right*, I first used this phrase to describe a capacity for knowing that comes through familiarity and attunement with our emotional reality. The capacity for knowing in depth *has* to include emotion as a medium of learning and knowledge about oneself and others. Fear of this medium will leave us with only a partial and superficial knowledge, which may get us through examinations but will never develop our capacity for wisdom.

We often refer to the battle between the head and the heart and we all know which side has more status in the real world. Once emotion has been released and clarity restored, it is possible to function emotionally *and* rationally concurrently, allowing for the reciprocal benefits of each facility, operating from the head and heart together.

16 | How emotions affect the body

*'Sorrow that hath no vent in tears
makes other organs weep'*

I HAVE never been able to discover who wrote these words but, clearly, at least one individual, a long time ago, was wise to the effect of lack of emotional release on the physical systems of the body. This wisdom remains as a fragment of popular belief that connects a particular emotional stress in someone's life with the onset of a physical illness. However, this belief assumes the status of an interesting but irrelevant connection when it comes to actual medical *treatment*.

A friend recently went to her GP because she had bronchitis. Around the anniversary of her husband's death a year before, concerned friends had asked her to stay with them, and so she had felt unable to shed tears openly and release the grief she felt especially acutely at that time. She suggested to her doctor that this was probably the reason for her bronchitis. His *personal* response was immediate agreement, saying the very same thing had happened to his own widowed mother not long before: his *professional* response was a prescription for antibiotics. The recognition that grief was connected with the illness could not extend to the possibility of encouraging the natural expression and release of her grief through tears. Wisdom has become eclipsed by scientific knowledge.

There is not one system in our bodies that remains unaffected by the arousal and persistent suppression of release of emotion. This chapter explores the connections between emotion and brain and body. We look at how emotional suppression impacts on physical health and the causes of psychosomatic illness in general, with particular focus on the effect of emotion on our immune system, digestion and respiration.

Unreleased emotion affects our physical health through body memories; through *somatisation* in which our bodies become the physical stage for our mental conflicts; through muscular tension; and through the effects of accumulated chemicals caused by continuous arousal of emotion *without* release.

Body Memories

Remember that at the point, already described, when a one-off or repeated experience of trauma is recorded in the memory, *everything* is stored there, including the physical impressions and perceptual information gained through the body's senses.

Sometimes, over the years, I have experienced quite dramatic evidence of these memories. During the course of massaging a woman who had come for general relief of tension to her neck and upper back, I found a particular place of discomfort on her right shoulder. As I worked to relieve this, she said softly, 'I'm embarrassed because for some reason I suddenly feel like crying.' With reassurance she was able to trust her body and release long-held and deep emotion. Together we found ourselves exploring a whole sequence of memories from when she was eight years old, a time when she would frequently return from school to a café where her mother was working. She would be met by her ill-tempered and harassed mother who regularly greeted her with a slap across her right shoulder as she entered the café. All those memories, set off by a caring touch in that one place on her body, had not been *consciously* recalled in many years.

The body remembers: fear held in the thighs after surgical investigations or experience of genital pain; anger held in body parts that have been touched intrusively or treated with contempt by others; grief held in parts that bear scars of loss or disfigurement. Sometimes these memories lead to tension and pain that have a knock-on effect on some other bodily system. At other times, we develop the physical equivalent of mental amnesia: a numbness and inability to respond to sensation because the unreleased psychosomatic pain simply becomes too much to bear.

Somatisation

The shift from mental numbness to physical numbness is one example of the way in which we 'translate' the language of the mind into the language of the body. We can also express *symbolically* the language of an internal and invisible mental conflict in an external, visible and physical form.

Two examples of this are anorexia and bulimia, both of which are related to the behaviour patterns in the engagement/containment polarity. The learning of the rules of aggression – power over or power under – involves the reversal rather than the resolution of conflict. The experience of being powerless at the hands of others, of being an object, convinces us that the only way to avoid this state is to become the one with power *over*. We can find someone else to make into the object so we can stop feeling powerless ourselves. However, in the absence of an arena in which to exert our own power through interaction with others, we use the only arena we have available – our bodies. The unreleased anger from earlier experiences is directed into aggression towards this object that is the apparent cause of our powerlessness.

In an anorexic context, the body becomes the object, separate from self so that instead of feeling at one with it, we feel at odds with it. Life becomes a continual struggle to conquer it. This object can be rewarded or punished at will – 'it' becomes my territory, my domain, my space over which I have absolute control. So we punish it: we mutilate it, starve it, stuff it, purge it and in doing so we believe we are saying 'No' to powerlessness.

Often this whole cycle is rooted in specific anger at being trapped within a female body which has to be controlled in order to conform to norms of attractiveness, in the same way that female behaviour has to conform to norms of attractiveness. Anger at the impossible unfairness of this situation – anger at the experience of the objectification of women – is aroused but unreleased. The longer the real but unattractive emotion of anger is stifled by self-punishing aggression, the more life threatening the conflict becomes – literally a fight between life and death.

The body becomes the *repository of blame* in all self-abusive behaviour. We punish ourselves by excess or inadequacy – too much or too little food, over-indulgence or neglect, excess work, alcohol or punitive renunciation of what would nourish us. Indiscriminate sexual activity – either unprotected sex or sex with individuals who treat us as objects – adds to self-loathing. Treating the body as an object, we can even cut off bits that offend with no more concern (probably less) than lopping an unsightly branch off a tree.

Aggression directed towards the self and the body can be seen again in bulimia. Bulimic behaviour is part of an adaptive pattern of response to unreleased anger aroused by insufficient experience of boundaries. One of the patterns described in Chapter 9 is becoming a *pleaser*. With bulimia, this extends to over-accommodation in terms of eating: bingeing, taking in anything and everything, unable to set limits and then spewing up, ridding ourselves of everything we have taken in unwillingly and compulsively. Everything we swallowed down to appear acceptable and acquiescent and pleasing comes forth with a huge relief and a sense of real power: the power to say a massive 'No', even belatedly.

With the spewing up comes the false self, the adapted nice self, the accommodating self and there is relief for a while: but what is left is emptiness. After the relief of disgorging all the acting and pretence, we see what lies underneath: the real person, the real self, who when seen through distorted perception appears ugly and disgusting. What makes this self appear ugly, i.e. fearsome, is our unreleased emotion: a powerful combination of rage and perceived powerlessness. And so the cycle continues into self-blame.

Muscular tension

My own working experience has taught me that the sites in the body connected to the struggle against emotional release can be grouped together under the three main areas of emotion, always allowing for individual variation.

The struggle against experiencing *grief* is generally located around the upper part of the body: tension accumulates in the lungs, the chest, the sternum and diaphragm. If you remember the process of sobbing, you can retrace the areas of primary tension. Because of the texture of grief, we can feel a lot of physical pain in these areas: stabbing, aching, piercing pains. In the short-term, choked back tears result in swollen glands, sore throats and headaches. In the long-term, the tension will spread beyond these areas, around the throat and eyes caused by habitual holding back or swallowing down. (In addition, I have found that the habit of swallowing back tears also leads to stomach problems such as an experience of acidity and difficulty in digestion.)

The sites of tension relevant to *anger* involve some of the most powerful muscles of our bodies: in our buttocks, thighs, calves, shoulders and upper arms. Tension in the pelvic area is mirrored in tension around the jaw. Release in one area triggers a corresponding release in the other. The process of struggling against anger can progress from acute pain in the head and neck and upper back to chronic pain over a period of time: migraines, lower back pain, inflammation of the sciatic nerve. Long-term effects also include wear and tear on the musculature of the heart.

The emotion of *fear* is also released through the jaw, so loosening up these muscles tends to facilitate first the release of fear that often leads to the release of anger. A common site of the tension of fear is in the musculature of the middle back and shoulders. Some of these muscles are also connected to nerve supplies to the stomach, so tension is caused in that organ as well. Anxiety affects our breathing apparatus which, in turn, affects the circulation of the blood.

Fear tends to promote rigidity or under-activity, anger promotes over-activity and spasm, grief promotes the experience of pain. As fear is usually the most accessible of all three emotions, defending us against the powerful feelings of anger which, in turn, defend us against the profound pain of grief, patterns of muscular tension are complex. It is never possible to point to a particular location of tension and give it one specific cause. This is not only the effect of overlapping emotional response but also related to other physical consequences, which have occurred or are occurring at the same time.

Cumulative effects of aroused and unreleased emotion

This aspect takes us into specialist areas of neural and biological science. Entering the realm of *bona fide* research is not always easy for the lay person because the subject matter is complex and usually assumes previous knowledge. What follows is a short dip into the vast pool of scientific information that demonstrates the existence and mechanics of an extraordinary communication system between the brain and the bodily systems with chemical substances functioning as messengers. It is less important to understand in detail how this system works, but the choice to learn to manage our emotions more effectively can be helped by the knowledge that the system does exist and is not part of our imagination.

Communication links between emotion, the brain and the body can be divided into three areas:

1. *The autonomic nervous system.* The best-known effect of emotional arousal on the body is seen through the function of the autonomic nervous system, which controls a number of important organs. The sympathetic branch of this system is responsible for what is popularly called the fight/flight response, in other words, readying the body to respond in either defence (anger) or escape (fear) with an increase in blood pressure, heart rate, etc. The blood is temporarily diverted from the digestive organs to the muscles and brain where it is needed for quick action. This is a normal biological response to the perception of danger. The body is given what it needs for emergency action: greatly increased levels of adrenaline and noradrenaline.

Problems occur when we perceive a threat that doesn't exist. Remembering the distorting effects of unreleased emotion, this is a common occurrence. Frequent bursts of noradrenaline lead to excess within the system: here it urges the heart muscles to work harder to increase oxygen supply, causing spasm or a heart attack if the coronary vessels are weak or blocked. Excess noradrenaline also contributes to the constriction of blood vessels and the formation of clots.

Apart from cardiovascular disease, this area of research suggests a whole host of illnesses associated with the effects of excess adrenaline/noradrenaline: headaches, digestive disorders, irritable bowel syndrome, sleep disorders and skin complaints caused by high levels of uric acid in the blood.

Overtly aggressive and hostile responses and their physiological effects are easily measured. However, much of the time, we are not aware of our feelings of anger, aggression or fear. This brings us to the second system of connection between mind and body: the structure of the brain.

2. *The structure of the brain.* The primary regulator – the 'control room' of emotional responses – is in the limbic system of the brain. This system is described as having its own kind of intelligence, rooted in primitive ancestral development. Information is sent from the limbic system to the hypothalamus and the cerebral cortex. The hypothalamus is responsible for influencing all the pituitary hormones that, in turn, control a massive network of other hormonal and biochemical processes in the body's organs. The

cerebral cortex governs cognitive learning and skilled behaviour regulation. Recent discoveries indicate that when information is transmitted from the body's senses, it is processed along parallel paths in the structure of the brain: cognitive and emotional content is sorted *separately*.

Between the limbic system and the cerebral cortex there is a constant interplay. The limbic system transmits the aroused emotion in response to a perception, urging a fast and primitive response. The cortex inhibits this impulse with a more rational and focused approach that often results in *lack* of evident emotional response. This encompasses occasions that demand appropriate emotional restraint and 'inhibition' so that we make a choice as to how to behave; more significantly, it becomes a generalised pattern of cortical activity when we have registered that *un*restrained emotional responses have met with negative consequences.

Learned inhibition makes it possible for a biochemical reaction to be triggered within the body in immediate response to the arousal of an emotion before the cortex acts to keep it out of conscious awareness. This means too that an overt unemotional response can mask all sorts of physiological activity, of which we are unaware because we literally cannot put it into words.

3. *Neuropeptides.* The third link is provided by the discovery of biochemical substances called neuropeptides. These are produced by nerve cells in the brain and communicate with their receptors that are located elsewhere in the brain, particularly in the limbic system, and throughout the body. Part of a highly complex system, neuropeptides constantly travel around the body and attach themselves to a specific receptor molecule: the receptors function as an information exchange for the body as a whole.

Having established that there is plenty of scientific knowledge to explain how emotions can influence the systems of the body, we now look at these connections in the context of psychosomatic illness.

Psychosomatic illness

The role of the emotions in susceptibility to certain illnesses has long been established in clinical circles. Yet, although diet, heredity and environmental pollution are accorded importance as contributory factors to illness, prevailing cultural attitudes prevent emotions from receiving the same attention.

First, the notion of psychosomatic – meaning of the mind *and* body – is confused with the imaginary. Many people are defensive about the suggestion that their illness is psychosomatic because the implication is that the illness is somehow in the head. This offends because it denies the very real pain or discomfort that people are suffering in their bodies and implies that they are malingering and could easily not be ill if they put their minds to it and generally pulled themselves together.

The following section looks at individual bodily systems to see how illness can be related to the experience of unreleased emotion, bearing in mind that the adaptations of one system will always impact on another. (Some of the research and further reading for this section is contained in the Appendix.)

Respiration and emotion. Asthma is one of the common illnesses believed to have an emotional component because asthma attacks can be provoked by a variety of emotions: joy, anger, anxiety, frustration. Emotional states affect the inhalation of allergens, making those already prone to asthma more sensitive. (See the Appendix for references to relevant research and other literature.)

Some theorists have suggested that asthmatic children and adults are more likely to bottle up their feelings and are more prone to anxiety than others, and it is not difficult to see how the struggle to keep back unreleased grief or anger or fear develops into an abnormal respiratory response.

Digestion and emotion. The entire intestinal system is lined with cells, including cells that contain neuropeptides and their receptors. When the sympathetic nervous system swings into action, its effect on the digestive system is twofold: in response to acute fear, it can increase activity to the point of diarrhoea or it decreases the activity of the whole gastrointestinal tract from the stomach to the lower bowel. When the system is slowed down, by a decrease in the supply of blood in order to concentrate bodily energy and resources on emergency action, constipation occurs.

Neuropeptide receptors are also found at the top of the spinal cord, where sensory information is taken in and processed by the brain. Muscular tension down the spine also directly affects the nerve supply to the stomach, the liver, the kidneys, the bowel through neural connections with the vertebrae.

When we have a sudden crisis, or bereavement or shock we are *aware* of not wanting to eat. When anxiety/rage/sadness become chronic and the feelings become detached from any recognisable source, the levels of chemicals in our blood cause disequilibrium in our mind–body feedback system. Any emotional arousal, even when we are not mentally aware of it, will hamper digestion. And yet, ironically, it is when we feel 'upset' or 'down' or 'tense' that we seek comfort and alleviation in the form of food. The aspect of food as symbolic of love, the encouragement to spoil ourselves with something sweet and starchy, the persuasion that a full stomach will compensate for feeling emotionally empty – all make it hard not to eat when we are emotional. Yet this is precisely the opposite of what we need to do for our health.

Even in the short-term, the intake of food, even 'healthy' food, into a system that is hampered by imbalance leads to all sorts of digestive difficulties. Wind, abdominal pain, constipation, diarrhoea are all acute disturbances but over time, symptoms can degenerate into colitis, irritable bowel syndrome, ulcerative colitis and duodenal ulcers, depending on individual susceptibilities and the contributory influence of diet. With the added factor of a weakened immune system, we can develop cancers of the digestive tract.

The skin and emotion. If an individual is susceptible to skin problems, then the high levels of uric acid in the blood associated with excess hormonal levels can contribute to eczema and dermatological problems. Sometimes the suffering caused by a skin disease, particularly if it adversely affects our appearance, can generate more emotion that further aggravates the situation.

The immune system and emotion. Another major effect of inappropriate levels of hormonal stimulation is on our immune system. Adrenaline in high levels is understood to suppress the immune system. Cortisol is another hormone produced in the adrenal cortex as part of the stress response. It acts as a kind of supercharger: it enhances the immune system, suspends allergic reaction while the body focus is on dealing with stress, and aids in wound healing.

Neuropeptides and their receptors play a vital part in the immune system. One main feature of the immune system is that its cells are constantly on the move. One type of cell, monocytes, which ingest foreign bodies, is responsible for tissue repair and healing wounds. They start life in the bone marrow and then disperse and travel in the blood through the circulatory system, their route guided by chemical cues. At some point they encounter a neuropeptide and because the monocytes have receptors for that neuropeptide on their cell surface, because they speak the same language as it were, they are attracted towards that chemical. The neuropeptides, with which the monocytes are 'communicating', are constantly affected by *emotion*, so disturbance caused by high emotional arousal and imbalance (caused by long-term suppression) will have a direct bearing on the outcome of this communication. Communication concerns how the body system will fight disease, how to detect a tumour cell and destroy it and which areas of the body need repair and restoration.

Once over-stimulation sets in, without the opportunity for the body to process the neurochemicals in the bloodstream, communication is distorted. The messages from the brain telling the body to respond to danger meets with the body's response that the current levels are already too high: this causes a battle during which the protection and maintenance of our immune system is weakened. This leaves us susceptible to minor illness such as colds and flu and coughs, and as this state becomes more chronic, leaves the body less able to detect rogue cells, thus leaving us more vulnerable to some kinds of cancer.

Management of emotion or a continued ostrich approach?

The bearing of emotion on the development of some types of cancer, especially breast cancer, has been studied quite extensively and links have been made with suppression of emotion. But as with other physical illnesses – asthma, arthritis, digestive disturbance, heart disease, skin problems, back pain and migraines – this is where the connection usually ends. The recognition of the link between emotion and illness is not extended to recommendations for further research and, most importantly, processing the emotions is not included in treatment of the disease.

In the past decade there has been a great deal of research and many words written and courses attended about dealing with stress. A lot of the physiological information is helpful in underlining that feelings actually have a real effect on the body but unfortunately, the term *stress* has become over-used and over-generalised to

include every emotion and feeling and state of tension and harassment that we experience as modern-day human beings.

I find it more helpful to think of stress as external factors with
which we have to contend in our living and working conditions:
traffic jams, noise, large masses of people, the need for speed, the
effects of artificial light, exposure to fumes, bureaucratic inefficien-
cy. What occurs internally and how these external stresses trigger
the responses that they do are more usefully divided into specific
areas of emotion and feeling which, as we have seen, have different
and specific effects.

The cultural assumption of good and bad feelings is implicit in
research studies and recommendations related to avoiding stress.
Anger, once again often confused with aggression, is proscribed as
a taboo emotion because of the link with cardiovascular disease.
This rules out the possibility of ever understanding the value of
anger. Similarly, other emotions are considered unhealthy because
of the deleterious effects of continuous arousal without release.

Because of the general injunction on expression and release, the
remedy is seen as avoiding arousal altogether rather than education
in *management* of feelings. The treatment of psychosomatic illness
therefore tends to go no further than reporting the links between
emotion and pathology but rarely considering the place of emotional management in treatment.

Obviously, emotion is only one factor that affects our health. The
individual route to good or bad health will always be a mixture of
our susceptibility – the genetic predisposition that we are born with
– and how this is affected, especially in our early years. Our basic
disposition is then subject to living conditions in adult life: exposure
to toxins, to infection, to viruses, diet, body maintenance through
lifestyle and outside stress factors all play their part.

My emphasis is on the emotional factor because the various
systems of the body cannot remain unaffected by the arousal and
persistent suppression of release of emotion. Until this link is properly researched and until it is seen that expression and release of
emotion can actually help alleviate or even prevent some illnesses,
the emotional factor will continue to be disregarded, confined to
cloud-cuckoo-land and approached with a view to avoidance.
Treatment will remain as incomplete as it would be if we ignored
any other equally important single factor. *Nothing will change until
we recognise appropriate release as a natural and health-restoring facility.*

◆ Are you aware of major illnesses, recurring ailments or injuries that you believe are connected with your psyche, even if you don't know quite how? Allow yourself to acknowledge that there is an emotional component. It doesn't matter if you don't fully understand it. Analysis is less important here than acknowledgement. This is the first stage in conveying to your body that you are prepared to listen to what it is communicating instead of suppressing it.

◆ Are you aware of dismissing and ignoring emotion by categorising it as merely a byproduct of hormonal activity?

◆ Have you punished your body in any way, by over-work, or over-eating or with insufficient attention, care and exercise? Make a note of these and see if you can link them with any particular feeling states.

17 | Living the mind–body link

WHAT relevance does catharsis have to normal, every-day life? People get on with their lives perfectly well without it. It's true that we can and do manage without too much exploration of our heartscapes. Many individuals who have suffered extreme traumas, even in their early years, manage to tran-scend their effects. Some people, for example are able to give to their children what they never received from their own parents and, in that loving exchange, find a way of healing their own wounds.

I believe that managing catharsis is relevant to our lives in many ways. First, there are occasions when catharsis just happens. This often occurs during a time of vulnerability: in response to a major stimulus such as a bereavement or shock, or when we are too tired to maintain the usual controls in place. We are also vulnerable at times of change when we often experience the beginnings of the release of feelings without any effort at all – they just emerge of their own accord. Unfortunately, instead of seeing this as the beginning of a vital and healthy process, we make an appointment with the doctor to get some treatment that will keep these feelings from going any further.

Any vulnerability, whether triggered by changes that are external (life events) or internal (hormonal), will leave us more open to emotions coming to the surface. When we are in a state of flux, our emotions, being psychosomatic, will be affected. The mistake many of us make is to blame the changes for causing the disturbance of emotion instead of understanding that the feelings which appear are *already there* (collected in our emotional ragbags), simply waiting for an opportunity to find acknowledgement, release and resolu-tion. Instead of seeing such an opportunity as the body's gift, we perceive it as a dangerous threat.

Familiarity with catharsis helps us to respond differently to these 'breakthrough' moments, to recognise and listen to the language of the body and appreciate its wisdom. When we suffer a deep loss, for example, we will probably find ourselves crying quite easily. Instead of suppressing these tears, we can permit ourselves, in private, to sob and howl, maybe many times over, because we know we need to. This knowledge can help to protect us from restrictive messages about being self-indulgent or childish and hysterical, which, otherwise, make us keep everything unnecessarily and often harmfully locked away.

A second way in which we become aware of the relevance of catharsis is through our bodies. There is a lot of available literature related to the symbolism of physical illness in relation to emotional problems so, by now, for many people, this is not an entirely new concept. The question is, however, what do you do about it? There is a world of difference between reading that your warts are residual manifestations of self hatred and actually knowing how to improve that particular mind–body link to your advantage. This is because we don't know how to experience the psychosomatic link deeply enough to release the emotion caught in the body; if we did know, we could improve our health at both levels simultaneously.

Catharsis is a key factor here. Rosie had chronic problems with her right hip. For years, her hip would mysteriously go out of place, causing intense pain, making her limp awkwardly and always necessitating a visit to the osteopath. This would remedy the problem – until the next time. With information about emotions and the use of catharsis, she was able to identify a pattern: the symptoms occurred whenever she felt very angry and frustrated. She experimented and found that she could detect the signs of tension in her body (lower back, buttocks, backs of her thighs) long before they registered in her head. She learned how to release some of the aroused feeling by kicking and shouting and generally letting rip and found that this eased the discomfort. In this way, she was able to prevent the tension getting to the point at which her hip would be pulled out of alignment.

Managing the mind–body link meant, for Maria, the start of a new relationship with food. She had known that her compulsive eating was somehow connected to feelings, but that wasn't enough to help her. The alternative to reaching for food, when she tried to stop herself, was the pain of unexpressed emotion. This was intolerable: she didn't understand what it meant and so she couldn't rationalise it away. What began as a temporary relief and comfort became a habit lasting for years. Information about feelings, and permission and encouragement to stay with them, helped Maria to be less frightened of them. She learned to detect emotional arousal just *before* she opened the cupboard or the fridge and to make herself stop for a minute and listen to her body in a different way. By staying with her 'emptiness' instead of denying it, she was able to acknowledge and release her feelings enough – to have a good cry or scream right there in the kitchen – to be able to start eating out of choice instead of compulsion.

The problem for many people at this point is, how do I start? How (and where) do I give myself permission to scream and shout and cry uninhibitedly? After so many years of mind over body and control from the neck down, how on earth do I begin to let go? At first the body – accustomed to being ignored over the years – will not co-operate. I remember, at the age of twenty-nine, in the middle of a week's course specially designed to introduce the skills of releasing emotion, being given permission for the first time to express anger. I opened my mouth to shout and not the slightest sound emerged. After so many years of keeping quiet, the muscles of my throat and jaw and chest and diaphragm had seized up and it took me a long while to re-educate my muscles to relax and for a genuine sound to come forth.

Rosie and Maria had attended such a course which is how they were able to apply what they had learned: skills in circumventing some of these bodily and rational controls, following body cues, moving with the breath, using volume to release psychosomatic tension. Some individuals find this easy to do for themselves; most people learn more effectively in the safe and structured environment of a course.

Why do people attend this kind of course? First, they may be aware of chronic illness or tiredness or bodily symptoms that persist despite all sorts of treatments. We have an *idea* that somewhere, somehow, the mind–body link is telling us something that we can't quite hear. We persist in seeking physical remedies and cures – doing the rounds of practitioners and diets and potions – focused on physiological alleviation. We may get near enough to the link to describe a backache or neck pain as 'stress-related'; we may suspect that a discharge or persistent joint problems are connected with conflicts in life, but that is usually the end of the story.

Second, an awareness of restimulation and its unhelpful effect on our current lives and relationships might persuade us to learn the skill of catharsis as part of a longer term strategy of emotional management. We may wish to lessen the effect of some of the unresolved situations from the past, to weaken the rigidity of some of the patterns and to respond more fully to emotion in the present. We may be aware of getting repeatedly stuck in the same old ruts in life but, even with the help of various kinds of counselling and therapy, have not yet managed to get to the root of the problems that continue to prevent us from experiencing fulfilment.

Learning the skills of adult catharsis requires a specific commitment. I was introduced to these skills through co-counselling (see Appendix) many years ago and practised them regularly in a structured context until they became a part of everyday life. These skills are immensely effective and useful for many people, but not everyone. I have adapted these skills into a wider context of management of feelings as outlined in the DANCE model. Basically, the aim is to help individuals to read and trust the language of their own bodies by recognising the correlation between muscular and emotional tensions. Specific techniques can help to subvert psychosomatic disorders. This kind of teaching differs from that which concentrates on analysis, cognitive processes or an intellectual understanding of emotion.

How long does it take to learn? A course teaching management of feelings is only an introduction and, given the number of years during which most of us have developed automatic physical and mental defences, it takes time to become comfortable and familiar with the expression and release of emotion. It *is* a start and it works, with practice, but it really entails taking a longer-term approach, especially if you want to investigate and release some of the emotions at the core of key patterns. The best way to conduct this kind of investigation is to make time to explore your heartscape, making the appropriate skills work for you.

These skills are not the prerogative of experts – they are part of normal mental health. You can incorporate the learning of them into your routine as you would with new language or new social skill. They require practice in trusting your body, trusting yourself to go *with* instead of *against* your body, even when you do not understand intellectually what is happening. You can learn to trust the body's signals and follow the syntax of the language of emotion when you are in an appropriate and safe environment.

Whether you are responding to what is emerging spontaneously or you actively want to explore your own heartscape more fully, here are some guidelines as to how and where release can safely and effectively occur.

Guidelines for catharsis

The need for safety

This is the first and a vital prerequisite. We have to feel safe. We have already looked at the paradox that describes the phenomenon of release of emotion only when the danger or perceived threat is past. We cannot release the emotion as long as the body's systems are required to function in a state of emergency or in order to ensure physical or psychological survival.

We need a context that is outside ordinary life, a safe space that is separate and private. Letting go of our normal controls and censorship is necessary for exploration and this requires privacy. Authentic catharsis is a private experience – we can shed a few tears and express some of the lighter levels of emotion in public without much harm, but catharsis needs privacy and safety.

There are two reasons for this. First, during the process of emotional arousal, as in sexual arousal, we lose touch temporarily with our hold on external reality as we become increasingly absorbed with internal bodily sensations. We stop *thinking* and our awareness of the outside world diminishes, though it never disappears completely. We need the safety of knowing that, for a short time, we can leave aside the roles and requirements of everyday functioning.

Second, travelling through our heartscape can be chaotic, unpredictable and messy. Things do not emerge in an orderly and rational manner because usually too much has been repressed and suppressed. Exploration takes us through intense and extreme places and, as we have seen, we become confused. This is a necessary part of the process and we cannot make sense of anything until the feelings are released and clarity restored.

What we say or do in the extremes of emotion need not be part of anyone else's experience. This is one aspect of emotional responsibility. It is irrelevant for others to see the part they play in our psychic meanderings. A neutral witness is able to be detached but there is no need for your child or partner to witness the hatred or despair of the four-year-old in you; there is no need for your parent to see your restimulated fury; there is no need for your friend to participate in an exploration of your jealousy and restimulated fear.

The need to take responsibility for restimulation

On many occasions when teaching assertiveness, I find that partici-pants first respond with over-zealousness. The pendulum swings from being passive to being aggressive (in the guise of being assertive) and it takes a while for real understanding to sink in. A similar behav-iour response occurs when people first learn skills in emotional man-agement. There is always a big temptation to ignore the dangers of over-zealousness because individuals persuade themselves that they know the difference between present and past (restimulated) emotion. They insist on expressing their feelings directly to a parent, for exam-ple, about their perceived past neglect, completely convinced that they can be emotionally clear. But they are fooling themselves.

Unfortunately, the deeply entangled threads of those unmet needs and longings of childhood distort the picture dangerously; the intensity of feeling and the interwoven child/adult perceptions make any kind of resolution highly unlikely. Anything locked away for too long tends to emanate an offensive smell. Although we tell ourselves that we are communicating as an adult, all the child's needs and longings and emotional intensity will creep in, leading to 'acting out' (see Chapters 9 and 12). The resulting behaviour is con-fusing and misleading and often extremely hurtful for the person on the receiving end. *You* might go off feeling relieved to have finally lost your temper after so long and be delighted to have got so much off your chest, but it is unlikely that you have communicated with-out 'dumping', i.e. leaving the other person buried under your offloaded pile of restimulated emotion.

It is impossible to communicate clearly during catharsis or dur-ing high emotional arousal, as we saw in Chapter 15. Certainly, the other person can pick up the emotional charge – that you are full of sorrow or rage – but clear communication with words is impossible. Resolution of any situation, past or present, remains out of reach until you can gain enough insight and clarity to take responsibility.

This means eschewing blame (however subtle or justified). One of the most addictive aspect of restimulated feeling is that it gives us a buzz; we really do get a kick out of it, whatever the mood – sulky, aggressive, hating, self-pitying, blaming, morose. It is so tempting and so much easier to hold on to this distorted energy than to take responsibility and to *let go* the aggression and the need to blame yourself or someone else. In my experience, this is one of the hardest decisions for most people to make.

We all have one or two favourite feelings – being powerless, aggrieved, confused, frightened, rejected, envious – that keep us wrapped in a familiar cocoon. It is more familiar and less of a risk to hold on tightly to those familiar feelings than to trace the feeling to its root, explore it and release the real emotion. If we did so, our perception would probably alter as a result of the catharsis and that would mean a considerable reshaping of what we need to believe about the past. This, in turn, would mean a considerable change in our own approach to the present and future. It would mean becoming emotionally responsible.

Emotional responsibility means choosing to process your feelings in private. It may be that you never communicate these things directly to the person concerned; or it may be that, at some point, you will tell them something. Realising that your feelings are *your* feelings and letting go of the need to seek compensation or revenge is what responsibility is all about.

The need for a loving witness

We need privacy to make it safe for others; we also need someone else there to make it safe for ourselves. At first, it is invaluable to explore with the help of someone I call a *loving witness*, a caring but neutral person who allows you to wander off and explore while they stand guard, as it were, holding the rope connecting you to the outside world. On your own you may either decide it is too unsafe to get started or, if you do wander off, you may be unable to find the way back. The reassurance of having a steady and caring presence nearby is the best policy.

Who can be a loving witness? Ideally, this is someone who has a working knowledge of emotional catharsis, such as a professional counsellor or therapist. It can equally be someone, like yourself, who has learned the relevant skills, and is interested in an exchange – being a witness for each other in turn. It could also be a friend, but this presents a difficulty. Having a good cry on the shoulder of a caring friend or partner is necessary and helpful at times, but it is virtually impossible for the other person to remain neutral. They may become too restimulated themselves or embarrassment may creep in, especially if it is a recurring pattern.

The boundary established by the neutrality of the other person is, in my experience, essential for real safety. We have seen many times how vulnerable we are, when emotionally 'undressed'; in order to explore our heartscape freely, we need to know we are not being judged or criticised. Most importantly, we need to have the space in which to explore parts of ourselves that we would not wish to be remembered and recounted in our ordinary lives.

The need for balance

Exploring this terrain, as I've said, is uncertain and unpredictable. You may find places that you will never want to approach too close-ly; places where you easily get bogged down and that you realise are best avoided; there are places from where the view is spectacu-lar and the air refreshing; there are places of quagmire, desert, fer-tility, calm and challenge.

Your heartscape can become a playground – a land of personal restoration, discovery and renewal. It is a place to which you can return when your perceptions become dulled with unidentifiable pollution, when your hearing becomes blocked with static interfer-ence, when your sense of yourself becomes fragmented and you feel disconnected from life, when you experience a heaviness and can-not intellectually find the reason why. Exploration of your heartscape can become an ordinary way of keeping yourself emo-tionally healthy in much the same way as you might monitor and take steps to care for your physical health, without it turning into an obsessive preoccupation.

Emotional expression and release need not and should not take over your life. With experience of dipping in and out of catharsis, you learn that it is not the anticipated plunge into the deep where you risk drowning; it is more like a series of tidal pools. If you are responding to emerging feelings, you can allow yourself, when safe, to let go and explore. You will know when you have explored enough and when it is time to re-emerge.

Your heartscape is best seen by moonlight. Long ago, I learned to settle for understanding by moonlight. Sometimes people make the mistake of wanting to reveal and analyse and expose *everything* in too bright a light so that, under pressure, some piece of the puzzle is forced into a place that it doesn't fit. We do this because it is easier to try to piece it all together exactly than to live with uncertainty.

The nature of this terrain is inexact. Our memories and images cannot be otherwise. Our perceptions, even if corroborated by others, cannot be proved. But in that inexactness, there is enough understanding to know the approximate truth for ourselves. We do not need to know everything exactly. We just need to know enough, to settle for seeing the landscape as if by moonlight, where we can detect the shapes and outlines, the general form and lie of the land, where the main dips and peaks and contours occur. We can see enough to negotiate safely and wisely even though some crevices and corners will never be touched by enough light to see in detail what is there.

Scrutinising every pebble and blade of grass mesmerises us and involves so much time and energy that it risks becoming a full-time occupation, leaving insufficient attention and energy available for relationships and tasks in the outside world. Too much focus on this interior landscape and we lose touch with what is currently stimulating and challenging and on offer to us; too little, and we fail to see clearly what is out there because our ability to be fully present in our relationships is blocked by unexpressed feelings and distorted perceptions.

The relationship between this interior heartscape and our external relational landscape has to be kept strong and effective, each nourishing and allowing for the development of the other. Whether you experience catharsis by accident (in the short-term) or more intentionally (longer-term exploration), communication becomes clearer and taking responsibility for your feelings becomes easier. Once you have sorted through your emotional ragbag *enough* with the cleansing assistance of catharsis, you are then able to express and communicate some of these feelings in order to enrich your relationships: to become closer, to be more honest with those who matter to you.

The need to return

The final aspect of safety is the need to 'zip up' again afterwards. Just as you need to remove some of your outer protection to explore and release emotion, so you will need to replace it when you are ready to return to the outside world with all the responsibilities, roles and masks you employ in everyday functioning. Having someone present helps with this important step: you need to return to your rational, everyday self, to be able to cope with 'normal' life. Exploration in release in any depth is possible only in a space specially created outside real life – this boundary is essential – so going in and coming back are equally important.

It is possible to incorporate a different approach to catharsis without investing in extensive therapy or losing touch with the demands of ordinary life. Not only can you learn to feel more at home with release of emotion yourself, but you can also feel more comfortable when a friend or colleague or partner or child is releasing emotion. From looking at how we can manage catharsis in our lives, we now turn to how this affects our approach to catharsis in others.

The role of loving witness for others

It often happens that we find ourselves with a child or partner or parent or friend or colleague or stranger who is in genuine distress and we want to help but we don't know how.

A loving witness must provide loving and unjudgemental attention as a gift to the other person, requiring nothing in return. It is when given this quality of attention that we experience the safety that lets us drop the normal masks and to risk expressing the inexpressible, to look at what frightens us.

Personal anxieties and concerns interfere with the ability to become a loving witness. Unless we are aware of them, they can make us behave in an unduly brusque manner or we may become over-involved.

What can I do? Nothing. If ever there was a case for just being, this is it. Because of anxiety, we try to forestall feelings by offering to get a stiff drink or rushing around to find tissues. In other words, we hasten to be active in some way when the best thing is simply to sit and wait, knowing that the other person is vulnerable and accepting this as a sign of their trust in you.

I don't know what's wrong. It doesn't matter. Probably the other person doesn't know exactly what's wrong either.

How can I make the other person feel better? Don't confuse the release of emotion with the pain of holding it all back. Relax. You do not need to sort anyone out or cure them of anything. Your presence is what is helpful, not advice or analysis.

I feel responsible. One of the great lessons that must be learned about other people's feelings is that they are *their* feelings, not caused by you.

I get too emotional myself. At first it is difficult to avoid being restimulated yourself, but you can learn to keep your attention as clear and unclouded as possible. The best and most effective way of learning how to be helpful to others in distress is to become familiar with managing your own catharsis. You will know then that your feelings are *your* feelings.

It frightens me when someone gets angry. We often get frightened by other people's anger, especially when we have difficulty in expressing our own. The volume of sound and the force of the emotion set off an alarm and it is difficult to keep clear, even when you know the anger is directed towards someone else. All you can do is to acknowledge your own anxiety and avoid *negating* the other person's feelings. Similarly to the previous concern, the more familiar and comfortable you become with your own anger, the easier this will be.

Recognition of someone's vulnerability does not require you to mollycoddle them but, after the release is over, it is useful to help them button up again, *this* is the time for the cup of tea or some strategy of revival or diversion.

Being a loving witness essentially comes from a balance between the heart and the head. The heart alone can be an obstacle to the necessary detachment; the head alone preoccupies us with trying to make sense of things. The balance allows us to respond to the other person in a way that gives them permission and safety but does not invade or transgress their boundaries.

The role of loving witness in a professional context

The role of a loving witness still applies when the situation happens to involve someone in a professional relationship. Even when counselling or therapy is not your responsibility, it is likely that you will encounter people in distress if you work in an educational, medical, legal or personnel environment.

If your specific work *is* in the field of therapy or mental health, your task may include analysis or advice or counselling but, when dealing with catharsis in a client or patient, the same quality of attention applies even though the equality is altered.

Trained professional counsellors, psychologists and therapists can still be uncomfortable with the release of emotion for all the reasons explored in this book. Apart from personal inhibitions, to which professionals are prone like any one else, I find that the biggest stumbling block is actually understanding the nature of catharsis and how to distinguish it from dramatisation.

Catharsis and dramatisation

In a culture that is basically anti-catharsis, the opportunity to release emotion is both frightening and appealing. In a variety of therapeutic and personal growth contexts, catharsis is encouraged in front of, or in the company of, large groups of people. This is often experienced as beneficial to the participants who value the release and consequent insights.

The opportunity is helpful but there is a risk of coercion. This can come from outside, through facilitators and other group members who confront an individual until she/he breaks down. It can also be coercion from within, a feeling that you have to demonstrate something to be seen as part of the group; that there is an emphasis on the release of some feelings rather than others.

Any kind of coercion is antipathetic to the natural route of catharsis, which will present something in a personal heartscape as and when that person is ready to address it. Things are occluded from consciousness because they are experienced as too threatening: defence against such feelings is a survivial mechanism. This is why we need to go at our own pace. It can happen that when pushed into dealing with a past experience prematurely, there will be some release, but rarely any insight enabling us to connect this release with patterns in everyday life.

Allied to coercion is the mistake of aiming to release something because we *think* we should. This applies both when we decide for ourselves and when someone else pushes us in a certain predetermined direction. Catharsis happens when the twin ingredients are present: safety and surprise. Surprise allows something to emerge, through the psychosomatic system, without conscious control. Without the element of surprise, what occurs is dramatised release, not genuine catharsis, because its very nature and momentum have been subjected to a linear rather than cyclic rule.

Mass catharsis sometimes takes us by surprise, offering a release of some kind. The sight and presence of other sobbing or screaming adults restimulates personal distress which prompts us to reinforce controls or be carried along with the general flow. Football crowds, musical and theatrical experiences, the 'theatre' of state marriages and funerals all generate a lot of restimulated emotion.

This is fairly harmless but differs essentially from chosen catharsis in private. There is very little understanding of restimulation in mass catharsis. Arousal of emotion will be triggered but there is no room for focused awareness or resolution because once the drama is over, the controls will be back in place. We rarely achieve any insight or take the opportunity to explore the relevance of the event to the content of our own emotional ragbags.

As long as we remain passive participants in an external drama, open to restimulation and possible manipulation, we don't have the chance to take responsibility for our emotions. This phenomenon is becoming exploited as cheap programme material by TV companies: individuals fight to participate in encounters designed to elicit and provoke the expression of feelings – with an abusive parent, for example, or a 'lost' member of the family. Audience ratings demonstrate that this kind of emotional display is hugely seductive.

It also highlights the difference between catharsis and dramatisation. Dramatisation is, as we would expect, a *display* of feeling, a conscious or unconscious *performance*. When learning the skills of catharsis, dramatisation can be a useful prelude to authentic catharsis. Such are the controls in our mind–body that we cannot go from total suppression and its legacy of muscular and mental rigidity to a state of open and fluid mind–body congruence in a single transition. It simply cannot happen. So, en route, it is necessary to dramatise a little to rehearse the body in order to retrain it to make sounds and so on, but this is only ever a way through the rigidity, never an end in itself.

There is no safety whatsoever in front of a TV audience. Participants will either be dramatising, using simulation as an understandable defence because of their basic vulnerability or, if some genuine release is experienced, they can be damaged while in that state, when there is no care or protection of any kind.

Unfortunately, our confusion about what is and is not catharsis allows us to mistake dramatisation for the real thing, even though there is a distinct difference in the quality of release. I have found that many of us know instinctively when someone is releasing emotion authentically: somehow it touches us differently and, even if restimulated ourselves, we can sense the need to protect the other person. Dramatisation tends to provoke a different response: we are not touched and sometimes feel irritated and impatient with someone who is simply stuck in a dramatised rut. But without experiencing catharsis ourselves, without awareness of the effect of restimulation, the distinction easily becomes blurred.

I have found that mental health practitioners are no more likely than anyone else to be alert to the difference between catharsis and dramatisation. Because of personal censorship and lack of familiarity with catharsis, it is easy to muddle the two. Sometimes we can become aware that someone is stuck in repetitive cycles but it is difficult to intervene effectively without being familiar with the process of release and the differing textures of the emotions.

It also, sadly, means that most professionals do not see the relevance or value of catharsis. Some will complain that they have seen individuals getting 'stuck' in catharsis and dismiss it as unhelpful, when, in fact, they are describing dramatisation. Others, who have lived through the last twenty-five years of change in the helping professions will remember the popular human potential movement which challenged conventional therapies. The fashion for encounter groups and heavily confrontational methods employed to help people break various addictions left many associating 'catharsis' with general emotional mayhem; a sometimes heavy-handed free-for-all with more than a few individuals bruised as a consequence. Again and again boundaries were not respected and dramatisation ruled.

Emotional management programmes

There is some sign of growing awareness – the need for children to grieve the loss of a parent, for example – but not many. I remember watching an art therapist working so movingly with a little girl who had lost her father in a terrorist attack in Northern Ireland. Through the specific drawing she was encouraged to remember, but as soon as her eyes filled with tears, the therapist discouraged her from releasing them. I was saddened that, unwittingly, the little girl was prevented from doing the one crucial thing she needed to do to heal – the very thing that her psychosomatic system spontaneously suggested.

In another instance, a young boy who had seen his mother fatally stabbed by her boyfriend understandably became a difficult child to place with foster parents. The first foster parents liked him and slowly, he began to trust them. Then, precisely because of this developing security, he began to grieve: he began to make sounds at night – keening, deep, anguished sounds – as he sobbed in his bed. This was his natural mind–body mechanism intact and working for him. Unfortunately, this wasn't how his foster parents saw and heard it.

They became anxious and, thinking he was 'disturbed,' asked for another home to be found for him. Restimulation and lack of understanding about emotional release prevented his grief being accepted and held.

There could be a place for emotional management (including catharsis) in treatment programmes for adults as well. There are many programmes for people suffering from depression, self-destructive behaviour, problems of addiction and eating disorders that rely very little on the value of catharsis. Most methods of counselling and therapy offer little training in actual emotional management.

The DANCE model can be useful in training participants in their own emotional management: how to identify and recognise what they are feeling, how to use self-disclosure and how to release emotion in a safe and appropriate environment when necessary. Many therapeutic programmes avoid an abreactive (cathartic) component because of its association with unmanageable chaos, whereas the DANCE model could be used very effectively as an educational and training programme to be taken by patients back into the world at large after treatment is complete.

At the level of information alone, practitioners may be able to use some of the ideas. Some of the key points can be summarised in the following reminders.

The predominance of aggression. This is part of the tendency to dramatise but it is important to see how easily aggression takes over a heartscape, rather like a prolific weed smothering the true emotions of anxiety, grief and especially anger.

The quest for sympathy. This is part of dramatisation and frequently occurs with clients in a therapeutic setting. Recognition of the need for balance between attention turned outwards and an internal focus can be really helpful in getting a client out of a rut.

The rhythm of catharsis. Understanding that this is fluid and that emotion is an *energy,* enables mental health practitioners to become more adept at 'juggling', at moving with the ups and downs of emotional energy in a patient; knowing when to intervene, or confront, or wait. It helps to be able to spot when there is a tendency towards premature closure instead of a real completion. Knowing when the cycle is over helps to ensure that the client is buttoned up again to face the outside world at the end of the working session.

A natural process. Truly understanding catharsis as a natural process allows the practitioner to intervene only when release is impeded in some way. There is no need to force or interfere through anxiety or impatience. The practitioner's presence is essential and his/her attention is essential because these provide the necessary safety, but this process requires a certain humility and respect in the face of what is an extraordinary human facility for self-healing.

Therapy or education? The over-riding obstacle I have faced with trying to incorporate management of feelings into an educational programme is the objection raised as soon as feelings are involved: 'But this is *therapy*, not education.' In our dualistic world, education and therapy become polarised. Of course, there are good reasons why therapeutic boundaries need to be established and therapy has a vital place in helping individuals to overcome or come to terms with their difficulties in life. However, alongside this reasoning, there is still an element of fear and ignorance about the nature of emotion. There is still a lack of familiarity with or understanding of catharsis that explains the professional eagerness to despatch any emotional matters hastily into the therapist's corner.

The past two decades have seen a shift towards an increasing dependence on professionals and away from self-help methods. Ordinary individuals are reluctant to process emotion because of the ingrained cultural conviction that feelings need a 'clinical context'. This stems from the realistic need for safety that I have already mentioned but it also, more obscurely, is related to an associated and less conscious need for someone expert, someone 'grown up', to make it better. The majority of adults stop processing their feelings when they are children – so that when they start again, for whatever reason, the 'mind-set' is that of a child. Old hurts and wounds restimulate old needs so that, as adults, we want our pain to be noticed and acknowledged because it wasn't at the time. I think this accounts for many adults' unwillingness to accept that the emergence of emotions connected to old hurts does not make them special in any way. Holding on too tightly to distress entails a corresponding holding on to the childish need for comfort, the need that wasn't met at the time. This need 'rationalises' the conviction that only a professional person can fulfil this function.

I have experienced personally the benefits of psychotherapy and yet I know that learning to manage my emotions and my familiarity with catharsis contributed greatly to what I gained from that experience. There are times when we need that particular boundary to establish dependence on a professional therapist, but I believe there are many ways in which we can learn to help ourselves as well. This, for me, is the importance of education. This information is something we can learn as usefully and naturally as we learn other subjects, as part of normal life instead of being associated only with having problems.

The DANCE approach is useful as education for adults but can easily be adapted for use with children and teenagers. Remembering the effects of faulty educational learning and its consequences can transform the way we relate to children either as parents or educators. Encouraging children to identify and name feelings, allowing them the safety to release emotion when it emerges, teaching the vital difference between necessary self-control and release without punishing the actual feeling are vital.

The box below shows a simple example of how some of the principles of emotional management might be incorporated into a child's educational package.

An Easy Guide To Feelings

All feelings are OK (contradicts the negative/positive dichotomy)

Learn the names of different feelings (helps to build a vocabulary of feelings and to understand the groupings)

Practise saying 'I feel' instead of 'You make me feel' (introducing the skill of self-disclosure)

Holding on to feelings too tightly for too long means they get out of hand (encourages expression and release)

Anybody can make mistakes: we all get feelings wrong sometimes (teaches discernment and introduces the possibility of restimulation)

Bad feelings are not your fault and you can learn from them (encourages acknowledgement rather than suppression of 'bad' feelings)

Expressing feelings helps you to understand yourself and other people better (reinforces the value of emotional communication)

Tears and shouting are best done when you feel safe and on home ground (teaches the need to release in an appropriate setting)

And, just for fun, here is an alphabet for adults:

Anger is a necessary emotion – aggression is a learned response

Bottling up leads to explosions

Coping with feelings tends to mean suppressing them

Denial of feelings doesn't help

Emotion is always moving

Feelings can be friends

General statements about feelings are not as effective as specific ones

Happiness is not an indication of self-worth

Intellectualisation of emotion ignores the body

Joy is what we feel when met as an equal

Knowing when we need to release emotion is part of the body's wisdom

Love and anger are both aspects of healthy relationships

Monitoring emotional health is as important as monitoring physical health

Naming the feeling stops it controlling you

Obstruction of emotion causes impoverishment at every level of being

Pain is what we feel when we struggle against emotion

Questions about others' feelings are wiser than assumptions

Risk sharing your feelings with a friend

Safety is essential

Tears release tension

Understanding feelings comes after release, not before

Voicing your feelings enriches your relationships

Worry goes round in futile circles

X-rated emotional outbursts are not for public consumption

Yielding to the process of catharsis is what it is all about

Zip up again emotionally when you're through

This chapter ends with a statement that, by now, will come as no surprise: the best way of learning how to work with emotion in others or to teach emotional management to others or to be comfortable with emotional expression, release and catharsis in a personal or professional capacity is through *learning to negotiate your personal heartscape and becoming comfortable with the mind–body process of catharsis in yourself.*

18 | Momentum: the impulse of emotion

Aꜰᴛᴇʀ considering the possibilities and practicalities of individual exploration, we look at emotion from a universal perspective, at its place in our lives. To understand emotion as potential energy, we need to step back from our individual heartscapes and take a wider view. The tradition of fear and ignorance about emotion has eclipsed the true nature and purpose of emotional energy.

This final chapter explores the motion of emotion. What are we responding to when we move towards closeness or safety at some times and towards engagement or risk at others? What is the energy that pulls us?

The word emotion signifies moving forth, moving out, the quality of movement is integral to its meaning. Our psyche and soma are constantly responsive to the ebb and flow of the three polarities: the impulse to move close – and the impulse to move apart; the impulse to break through a barrier – and the impulse to be contained by a firm boundary; the impulse to retreat into safety – and the impulse to risk the unknown. We move back and forth, sometimes strongly, at other times more gently, as we might respond to underlying currents in the ocean.

In addition, we are subject to the momentum of emotion between the three polarities from three different and separate sources: *intra*-personal, *inter*-personal and *im*-personal.

Intra-personal. This is the basic raw material, the source which lies *within* the individual. It is the deepest and most fundamental source of emotion, seen in its essential form in the instinctual animal part of our being which is shaped and refined through human development. From these instinctual roots arises our crude emotional raw material. The primal source of emotion tends to recede as we develop more sophisticated human capacities, but it remains to inform our behaviour and emotions throughout in our lives.

Primary emotions of love inform and form the fabric of family bonds, intimate companionship, the comfort of skin contact. As instinct is part of our loving, it is also part of our grieving: a mother who suffers the death of her child, especially when the death is sudden and terrible, will often respond with a wild seemingly 'crazed' grief and utter strange, 'non-human' sounds of pain that we can also hear in the cries of animals when they have lost their young.

Primary emotions fuel the immediate 'gut' sense of outrage when someone puts up a fence on *your* side of the boundary, takes *your* place by the pool, parks in *your* place, tidies *your* desk for you, sleeps with *your* wife! Add to that the pack instinct, and we understand how gang warfare occurs and even how international warfare is glorified. War is usually about territory. More recently, the car has come to represent personal territory. Behind the wheel when conditions are stressful, many drivers exhibit primitive and maniacal aggression towards others who infringe *their* space on the road.

Fear will incite a group of humans to stampede like cattle. The panic in a crisis, such as a fire, or accident on board ship, or any incident when people have to fight for their lives, often prompts primal behaviour, pushing everyone else out of the way. We describe a state of intense fear by comparison with a rabbit immobilised by headlights; any human who experiences prolonged exposure to fear will exhibit a similar paralysis.

The intra-personal impulse is the *root* impulse of emotion. Without the instinct to nurture and to bond and the corresponding loss, we would feel no love or sorrow. The instinct to play and for hostile display are integral parts of our own emotions of joy and corresponding anger when our boundaries are infringed. The animal instincts of fear and trust inform what we refer to as a gut instinct that either warns us of danger from another person or situation, or 'tells' us that someone is safe and trustworthy.

This root impulse of emotion constitutes a power within individuals. I see it as providing three potential life-energies associated with the three polarities: the fundamental urges to create, to exert our will and to explore.

1. *Creativity* is seen throughout the animal world in patterns of mating, generating, building; at a human level it is seen in our capacity for creative thinking, action and imagination. Culturally, the word 'creative' has come to be narrowly defined in terms of

individual accomplishments and 'works of art'. But there is an infinitely wider possibility open to us all: the potential to breathe life into matter, to create with a variety of components or ingredients – food, fabric, words, rhythm, ideas, sounds, seeds, metals, clay, colours.

This potential occupies us with initiating, growing, setting in motion, forming, generating, organising, ordering, making a new shape or form. This may be an individual enterprise, or a process of creative fusion with another or a group: singing in a choir, conceiving and executing an embroidery project, starting a team project, parenthood, planning a new home together.

2. *Challenge* describes our fundamental urge to exert and impose our will on our environment. The capacity urges us to change, to remove a hindrance, to subvert a restriction. The energy required to build a beaver's dam is echoed in our own desire to harness the elements of earth, water and fire to suit our own purposes, to adapt our surroundings.

3. *Curiosity* is a timeless drive that is part of our biological inheritance: the impulse to sniff out, to unearth, to negotiate unknown territory. We need to find out how things work, to take things to pieces, to analyse, to research, to find explanations. We have a profound and universal desire to understand. The quest for knowledge has resulted in both ordinary achievement – tying your own shoelaces, working the video, looking up the meaning of a word – and *extra*ordinary achievement. The compilation of a dictionary, a compendium of flora and fauna, the repertoire of homoeopathic remedies, voyages of discovery, the splitting of the atom – just some examples of the dedication and scholarship of a few humans urged on by their own curiosity.

It is important to remember that these three urges, these three life-energies, are inter-dependent. They are three distinct strands but, in reality, it is hard to separate one from another. Achievements such as overcoming our lack of wings by inventing an aeroplane or devising technology that crosses the barriers of time and distance illustrate this inter-dependence. The invention of cosmetic surgery, amphibious vehicles, explosives, insecticides and refrigeration are just further examples of our human urge to say a resolute 'No' to the inevitability of natural forces as well as evidence of our urge to understand combined with our creative imagination.

Inter-personal. This second source, the middle layer, so to speak, is the one of which we are most conscious. It describes emotion that arises from contact *between* individuals. As we move in response to our impulses, we find ourselves *in relationship* to others. From the moment of birth and beforehand (given the more recent understanding of inter-uterine experience), we are constantly subject to interaction with other human beings.

We are affected by all those with whom we come into contact as we attempt to meet our needs and to follow our own rhythms. Our needs for closeness and separateness, engagement and containment, safety and risk will be fulfilled at times, neglected at others, and we encounter all sorts of emotions to a greater or lesser intensity throughout our lives.

The interactive source is the reactive impulse of emotion: it is generated by our *reaction* to all the others we encounter in our lives. Interaction with others not only refers to literal others, but applies to all the people, real or fictional, who influence us for better or for worse along the way. It encompasses all the significant people who play a part in the interweaving of our lives. The feelings we experience are triggered by the dynamic of relationship. Whom we meet, how we meet, when we meet, the entire cycle of encounters small and large, meaningless and meaningful, will affect our needs and therefore our emotions.

The interactive material of our lives will depend on personality and particular life experience. There is, however, one final ingredient that affects us regardless of personal circumstance, rather as the overall climate affects the growth and development of a single tree.

Impersonal. This third source of emotion is *beyond* the individual. It includes all those phenomena which have a great and often drastic effect on our lives but which are beyond the dimension of personal interaction and relationship. It relates to a further dimension of experience in our lives: exposure to a vast range of stimuli and events that have little to do with our personal circumstances.

All sorts of things happen *to* us indiscriminately. These are the impersonal and sudden triggers of emotion: earthquakes, typhoons, floods, plane-crashes, random violence, discoveries of oil or gold, avalanches, eruptions, stock market collapses. Any such occurrence can affect our needs on a minor or major scale: freak weather may kill off your home-grown tomatoes or ruin someone's livelihood by devastating an entire crop of vines.

We are also constantly exposed to the less dramatic but profound long-term effects of social and political change, of climatic and geographical change that take no heed of the individual. Yet, exposure to these phenomena affects us *emotionally* because they will have an impact on whether or not our needs and impulses are fulfilled. We are subject to these external forces and influences even if we are not aware of them.

The character we inherit, the genetic legacy that promotes certain tendencies and sensitivities, will help to form the whole psychosomatic potential within each of us when we are born. How the *intra*-personal material is shaped will depend on what occurs in response to all those we encounter in our lives, in other words, the particular *inter*-personal experience. This is responsible for the ultimate form and expression of the *intra*-personal material – whether it is reduced, expanded, enhanced, hidden, subdued, stifled, celebrated or suppressed.

The *intra*-personal interacts with the *inter*-personal, which interacts with the *im*personal. All in all, the combination of streams which change according to life events, age, stage, and the wider movements of the world in which we live are *always* and *for ever* in motion. There are times when we deliberately impose an event on ourselves, when we consciously decide to change course and there are times when events occur unpredictably. The main emotional currents can be gentle or strong, the pull in one direction or another dominating at different times in our lives.

This is why a favourite metaphor for emotion is the ocean – precisely because it is in a constant state of flux, with times of violent movement, times of tranquillity, but never fixed: even when frozen on the surface, at depth it remains fluid.

Amid this constant movement is a point of emotional and physical balance, connected to and holding the individual human; a timeless weight acting as an anchor for the self, offering a point of steadiness, stillness and consolidation. How we can regain and retain this balance and learn to ride the currents of the heart with recognition and awareness instead of fear is what this book has been all about.

Appendix

Setting the scene

If you choose to do these exercises with someone else, the other person clearly needs to be somebody you trust. Trust will depend on safety; safety will depend on the following equally essential factors.

1. The first and most obvious factor is that you need someone with whom you are able to be yourself.

2. Reciprocity: only when each person takes a turn to explore these exercises will there be a balanced give and take of time and attention. This is essential for safety.

3. Boundaries: related to reciprocity is the safety of structure. This involves setting time aside from *any* other activity whether working, personal or social. It also involves making a specific space in which this exchange can happen, and allocating a specific time (30–60 minutes is recommended), shared equally. It is also important as part of the structure that whoever is not talking learns to listen without interfering, advising or counselling. There is no need to talk. (See discussion of the 'loving witness' in Chapter 17 page 172.)

4. Confidentiality: clearly it is crucial that you establish an agreement that whatever is shared is done so in confidence.

If any *one* of these factors is missing, you will be unable to establish enough safety to get the best out of the exercises together.

These recommendations concerning all four aspects of safety would apply equally to two, three, or more people working together.

Psychosomatic illness

There is copious literature and research on psychosomatic illness (in contrast to the paucity of investigation into how positively to affect the outcome of the psychosomatic link for the patient). Below is a tiny sample of what is available:

- Thomas Nielsen at the Institute of Psychology, University of Arhus, Denmark, has written a fascinating paper called 'Mind and Body in Western Psychosomatic Research' and also a book *Psyke og Cancer* (Psyche and Cancer), 1994. Some of the research I found helpful includes:

- Samuel I. Cohen, *'Psychological Factors'*, in *Asthma* edited by T. Clark (Chapman and Hall, 1977).

- G. Mandler, *Mind and Emotion* (New York: Wiley & Sons, 1975).

- Joseph. E. Le Doux, 'Sensory Systems and Emotion: A Model of Affective Processing', *Integrative Psychiatry* 4, 237–48 (1986).

- Joseph E. Le Doux, 'Cognitive–Emotional Interactions in the Brain', *Cognition and Emotion* 3 (4), 267–89 (1989).

- Professor Terry Looker, *The Pathophysiology of Anger* paper (Department of Biological Sciences, Manchester Metropolitan University).

- Candace Pert, *The Molecules of Emotion* (London: Simon & Schuster, 1998).

Co-counselling

Co-counselling is a method of teaching skills with the primary intention of releasing emotion. Originating in Seattle over thirty years ago, the movement of Re-evaluation Counselling (RC) spread to much of the world. RC communities sprang up with individuals selected to become teachers of 'fundamental' classes. This refers to a 20–30 hour programme which supplies the fundamental training. A student typically attends such a class and then is able to continue to use these skills with another similarly trained individual, exchanging time equally.

The originator was Harvey Jackins who headed a hierarchical organisation of carefully selected teachers. In the mid-1970s, some of his teachers broke away to form an independent community (CCI). The intention was to promote a more democratic and less top-heavy power structure. While still teaching the same skills, bodywork and techniques from other disciplines became part of the co-counsellor's 'repertoire'.

I was introduced to co-counselling through CCI during its first breakaway year. The reciprocity of the structure (each person taking equal time in turns to be client and counsellor), the emphasis on self-empowerment rather than dependence on outside expertise and the focus on the body instead of analysis combined to offer me something that I knew I could and would use for the rest of my life.

My enthusiasm led to my teaching co-counselling and establishing a community in London. My involvement continued for many years but eventually I became frustrated with the lack of consciousness about the realities of sexism, heterosexism and racism both at an individual and community level. I withdrew from active participation although always maintaining my personal practice and commitment to the concepts and skills.

In the continuing RC movement, there was a much greater commitment to such social issues but the 'breakaway' group was still officially considered as a traitor to the cause and little dialogue was possible between the two branches. The perpendicular power structure also continued, and continues, to hold sway.

One of my main concerns, both as a teacher and as a co-counsellor, was the tendency to see emotion as something to be kept separate from life and only sorted out/worked through in a session. Obviously, privacy is a necessary part of management, but what I missed was the ordinariness of emotion. Restimulated emotion needs a private context to be sifted through, but what about acknowledgement and self-disclosure every day of one's life? Where was the place for emotion in the context of a daily relationship? This motivated me to devise the DANCE approach: first, so that catharsis could be just one part of emotional management, not the entire aim. Second, to emphasise the need for clear ongoing links between catharsis, insight and *real* life, instead of a tendency to become overly focused on the personal and thus, consequently, blinkered about the social and political.

With these provisos, there are still good teachers in both communities. Attending a fundamentals course is the best way to be introduced to the skills of catharsis. Any interested reader can contact a local RC community or contact John Talbut, the current CCI contact person in the UK, who also has information about CCI worldwide. He can be contacted at The Laurels, Berry Hill Lane, Donington le Heath, Coalville, LE67 2FB: tel/fax 01530 836780, e-mail John@dpets.demon.co.uk. Internet: www.co-counselling.org.

My comments and historical observations are clearly personal and I would recommend reading more about the history and concepts of co-counselling from other sources:

- Rose Evison and Richard Horobin, *How to Change Yourself and Your World* (Co-counselling, Phoenix, 1990).
- CCI internet website: http://www.dpets.demon.co.uk/cciuk
- John Heron, *Feeling and Personhood* (Sage Publications, 1992).
- Re-evaluation counselling has a quarterly publication, *Present Time*, containing news about RC worldwide. Contact Roland Matthews, 70 Winchester Road, Romsey, Hants, or Rational Island Publishers, 719 2nd Ave North, Seattle, WA 98109, USA.

Sources

I was introduced to the way feelings can be divided into three groups around the emotions of love, anger and fear through co-counselling theory: the terms 'pattern' in this context and 'restimulation' also come from co-counselling.

At various places in the book, I have referred to suppression, repression, 'splitting' between good and bad emotions and infantile fantasies. These clearly are part of the wealth of classic psychoanalytic literature.

The three complementary polarities, the patterns related to these polarities, the textures of release, the distinction between anger and aggression, the momentum of emotion with its three impulses, the difference between emotion and feeling, the concept of 'kites' and the DANCE approach are all part of my own thinking, experience and chart-making.

Index

Accumulation 106, 107, 129–35
Acknowledgement 106, 111–21, 138, 145–6, 166
Adaptation 81, 82, 84–5; acute 85; permanent 85; cycles of 85–7
Adrenaline,excess 159
Affect 3
Aggression; and anger 19–20, 92–3, 156, 164; and fear 99; and catharsis 133, 134, 180
Alcohol 8
Anger; and aggression 19–20, 92–3; value of 5, 25, 164; emotional patterns and 91–6; release of 59–60, 140; as primary emotion 112–3, 186; trapped 150; and body memories 155; and eating disorders 156–7; and physical sites of tension 157–8
Anorexia 156
Anxiety, chronic 97, 119, 149
Apology 114
Appropriate emotions 7
Arousal; emotional 51–7, 67, 72, 74, 78–9, 170
Asthma 161
Autonomic nervous system 159
Avoidance 87

Balance, catharsis and 173–4
Behaviour; self-defeating 95; abusive 95–6; human patterns of 100–1, 137, 149–51
Blame 93, 116, 156, 171–2
Blocked emotional energy 70–1, 131–2
Blocked insight 136–7
Body memories 155
Boredom 117
Brain, and emotions 159–60
Bulimia 156, 157
Breakthrough moments 166–7

Cancer, and emotions 163
Carer patterns 90
Catharsis 106, 129–35, 136, 137, 145–6, 166–84; mass 177–8; and dramatisation 178–9; rhythm of 180–1
Challenge 187

Changes, and emotions 27, 54–5
Childhood experiences 28, 29; and three polarities 30–42; unmet needs in 47
Choice, behaviour and 152–3
Closeness, need for 13–16; experiences that meet need for 14; experiences that block need for 15; in childhood 30–3; and grief 58–9; and emotional patterns 87–91; emotions associated with 113–5
Coastliners 26, 27
Coercion, catharsis and, 177
Cognitive distortions 79
Cognitive patterns 86–7
Collusive behaviour 94
Communication links, brain and body 159–60
Compassion 16, 114
Completion, release and 59, 60, 61, 65
Concealment 87
Confidence 120
Containment, need for 13, 17; experiences which meet need for 18; experiences which block need for 19; in childhood 33–7; and emotional patterns 91–6, 156; emotions associated with 115–9
Control, of emotions 64–6; fear of losing 146
Cortisol 162
Creativity 186–7
Crisis 62
Cultural conditioning; and emotional divisions 4–8, 111, 164; tolerance of emotional display and 7–8; and separateness 14; and fear 23; and control 65–6; and social behaviour 151
Curiosity 187
Cycles, completion of 45; of arousal and distortion 79–80; of repetitive behaviour 83–4

Denial 106, 107, 109–110; emotional 8, 87
Depression 94–5, 118–9
Digestion, and emotion 161–2
Disappointment 116
Distorted perceptions 76, 126–7
Distortion 106, 107, 136–41, 149
Distress 106, 109–110, 145–6

Dramatisation 178–9
Dumping, restimulation and 171

Embarrassment 120
Emotion, nature and purpose of 55, 67, 75–6, 185–9
Emotional cores 150–1
Emotional development 49
Emotional display 7–8
Emotional dispositions 26, 27
Emotional education 47, 78, 105–6, 145; direct instruction and 47–8, 65–6; indirect absorption 48–9, 65–6; blocked 70–1
Emotional management 110, 179–82
Emotional release 58–62, 63–71, 85, 128, 129–35, 154–64
Emotional response 51–5, 85; pure 71
Emotional tension 67–72
Emotions; categorisation of 4–8; co-existence of 5–6; rationalising away 6–7; trusting 8; basic areas of 11–25; and feelings 111–21; understanding 145
Endings 45
Energy, transforming blocked 139–41, 185–9
Engagement, need for 13, 17; experiences that meet need for 17–18; experiences that block need for 18–19; in child-hood 33–7; and emotional patterns 91–6, 156; emotions associated with 115–9
Envy 116
Equality 19–20
Evaluation 106, 136–41, 145–6
Evasion 106, 107, 122–8
Exaggeration 87

Fear 22–4, 25, 41; of emotional release 65–6; emotional patterns and 97–100; as primary emotion 112–3, 186; and catharsis 133, 134, 140; and fantasy 146; trapped 151; and body memories 155; physical sites of tension 158
Feelings 3; as responses to experience 23; releasing 42, 46; and emotions 111–21; acknowledging 121; communicating 138; guide to 182; alphabet 183
Fight/flight response 159
Food 28
Fragility 118
Frequency. stimulus and 29
Fulfilment 117

Grief 14, 15; usefulness of 25; and blocked childhood needs 33; release of 58–9, 140; emotional patterns and 87–8, 90; as primary emotion 112–3, 186; trapped 150; and body memories 155; physical sites of tesnion 157
Guilt 115–6

Happiness 5, 115
Heartscapes 26; formation of 27; childhood and 28; dealing with emotions and 41–2; exploring personal 102, 169–75
Humiliation 117–8
Humour 3

Imagination 152
Imitation, learning and 48–9
Immune system, and emotion 162–3
Impact, need for 59
Impersonal, the 188–9
Inequality,and aggression 20
Inhibition 80
Inlanders 26–7
Insight 136–8, 171
Intellectual clarity 149–50
Inter-personal, the 187–8, 189
Intra-personal, the 185–7, 189

Jealousy 120–1
Joy 18, 20, 25, 150

Knowing, emotional intelligence and 153

Laughter 68–9
Life energies 186–7
Loneliness 120
Loner behaviour 89
Love 13, 14, 25, 28, 31, 150
Loving witness, the 172–3; being for others 175–6; professional 176

Manipulative patterns 99–100
Memories; of pre-verbal experiences 43–4; and restimulation 72–3; and blocked emotions 76, 78, 84, 149
Mental amnesia 155
Mental conflict 156
Mind–Body link, managing the 166–84
Monocytes 162–3
Mood 3
Muscular tension 155, 157–8

Naming 106, 122–8, 138, 145–6
Needs, met and unmet 28, 55, 87–100; blocked 84

Negative feelings 4–5, 6–8; and isolation 6; and three polarities 12, 15, 16, 19, 22, 32, 37, 41; suppression of 80
Neuropeptides 160, 161, 162, 163
Nourishment 11, 12, 13

Obligations, fulfilling 64
Oppression; and aggression 20; emotional 46

Patterns, emotional 85–7, 90–101, 150–1
Passion 3
Peace 117
Perception, process of 51–5; and arousal 52–7; and emotions 75–6; distortion and 76
Physical; and psychological needs 28; release 67–8; health and unreleased emotion 154–64
Physiological; insight 129, 136–8; release 129–31
Pity 114–5
Positive feelings 4–5, 8; and three polarities 15, 18, 22, 31, 35, 39; frozen 80
Pride 117
Primal experiences 44
Primary emotions, the 112–3
Psychological boundaries 13
Psychosomatic; balance 42, 67, 75–6; release 42, 45, 56–7, 61, 140, 146–7; mechanisms 53, 63; arousal 53; tension 55, 61, 67–72, 74, 125, 132–4; blocks 70–1, 139–40; connections 109–110, 145–6; illness 154, 160–4

Rationalisation 106, 107, 111–21
Reason, and emotion 6–8
Regret 114
Rejection 116–7
Release; sexual 56–7; emotional 56–62, 67–72, 75–6, 129–35, 161; physical 67–8; mental 68; diversion and 68–70; and self-disclosure 125
Resolution, point of 61
Respiration 161
Responsibility; and choices 152; for restimulation 171–2
Restimulation 71–81, 126–8, 171–2; and distortion 139, 140–1, 149
Return, catharsis and 174–5
Rhythm; of grief 58–9; of anger 59–60; of fear 60–1; of laughter 69
Risk, need for 13, 23; experiences which meet the need for 22; experiences

which block the need for 23; in childhood 37–42; emotional patterns and 96–100; emotions associated with 119–21

Self; blame 79, 157; control 99; images 89; pity 115; disclosure 122–6; loathing 156
Sentiment 3–4
Separateness 13–16; experiences which meet need for 14–15; experiences which block need for 15–16; in childhood 30–3; and emotional patterns 87–91; emotions associated with 113–5
Sexual arousal 52–4, 69, 72, 170
Shame 116
Shut down 135
Singing 69
Skin, emotions and 162
Somatic accumulation 76
Somatisation 154–7
Sorrow 16, 114
Sound; of grief 58–9; of anger 59–60; of fear 60
Stimulus 29, 45, 126–7
Stupidity 120
Suppression, emotional 46–7, 70–1, 154–64
Surprise, catharsis and 177
Survival 11–13; patterns 81–101
Suspension, emotional 44–5, 63–5, 78
Sympathy, quest for 134–5, 180

Tension sites 157–8
Therapy, self-help and 181–2
Three polarities 13–25, 55; balancing 23; moving along 28; childhood and 30–42; blocked emotions and 87–100; life energies and 186–7
Tides, emotional 26
Trauma, early life 44 45
Trust 13; and environment 21; and risk and safety 22, 35; value of 25; trapped 151

Vanity 89
Vicariousness 98
Vulnerability 114; of infant 28, 29, 42, 46; and emotional arousal 54–5; release and 69, 166; and adaptations 85

Wheel, as image of emotional patterns 85–7, 149–51
Worry 119–20